The Lonely Now

by NICKY CRUZ

as told to Jamie Buckingham

ILLUSTRATIONS BY JIM HOWARD
PHOTOS BY KEITH WEGEMAN
AND
STITT — COOMBS — EVANS INC.

Charisma Books
Box 292
Watchung, N.J., 07061

© copyright 1971 by
Logos International
Plainfield, New Jersey
All rights reserved
Printed in the United States of America

Library of Congress number 72-95766
SBN 912106-15-8

Second Printing, March 1971

Special Charisma Edition 1972

To my daughters
ALICIA, LAURA, and NICOLE.
My prayer is that they will never
be part of *The Lonely Now*.

Contents

Introduction

Nov. 28, 1970

Dear Nicky:

Consider me your Number One Fan. As you know, I leaped at the opportunity to make a television special with you after reading *Run, Baby Run,* and I will never forget the exciting days we had together while filming this extraordinary story of your conversion, and the crusade you have led against drug abuse ever since.

Now comes this powerful "inside" book *The Lonely Now,* which, to my mind, is a bloodcurdling cry for help from the tens of thousands, perhaps even millions, of forsaken, desperate, ignorant, and suicidal people in our country.

During this past year, since we lost Diane to the curse of an LSD flashback, I have traveled across the United States many times, speaking, listening, watching, and learning about the terrible epidemic that is threatening our young people. Many times, I have said to my audiences, "I wish I could take you with me into the ghetto, into the subculture of our youthful drug addicts, and into the minds of the curious, rebellious youth who are risking everything for a momentary thrill."

Now, with this book, you have given the reader just that opportunity: to look into the lonesome hearts of the kids who are turning to drugs, sex, crime, and perversion because their lives seem empty—kids who have a "hole of loneliness" in their souls.

I, too, have received over 100,000 letters from concerned people frantic over the tragedy on our doorstep. But most of my communications were from parents wanting to know what to do to save their children.

Your letters are from the kids themselves, and reveal in stark, personal terms why so many of them are "turning off" their parents and "turning on" with the synthetic thrills afforded by chemistry and illicit love.

And your answers are so true . . . your advice so solid . . . your conviction so strong, that the entire book becomes a dramatic sermon, vividly reminding us of the importance of Jesus Christ as a living Savior, and offering the one, final answer to our tragic problems.

ART LINKLETTER

1

"Please Help Me!"

East Village, New York City. The home of the hippie.

It was midnight and St. Mark's Place was crowded with the weird, the freaks, the dirty, the unshaven. They thronged the sidewalks and spilled out into the streets.

I had come back to New York on the invitation of Billy Graham, to share my testimony during his New York Crusade at Shea Stadium. I had arrived a day early because I wanted to visit some of my old haunts in Brooklyn and explore the teenage hangouts in East Village. Gloria was with me.

"If you want to see what East Village is all about, go to the Electric Circus," I had been told. And so we went.

Gloria has ministered with me in many difficult situations since our marriage. We've lived in the ghettos and worked with drug addicts, runaway children, dope pushers, and sex perverts. Yet she was not prepared for what we encountered inside the Electric Circus.

The flashing strobe lights and whirling psychedelic colors picked out the hundreds of writhing bodies grunting and twisting to the ear-shattering, pulsating beat of a combo known as "The Grateful Dead." Huge murals of naked men and women in lewd poses leered at us from the walls.

"God created angels and died," the inscription read.

THE LONELY NOW

In a side room, couples lay on the floor. In front of us, a boy let his hands roam over his male companion, much to the delight of several other homosexual teenagers who were urging him on. On the steps, as we left, two under-twenty girls embraced tightly—mouth to mouth.

Outside, homeless, lonely youth, dressed in costumes that ranged from amusing to absurd, walked back and forth as if participating in some kind of ghastly Halloween parade. Back and forth, back and forth, back and forth . . . like caged animals in the zoo.

A young couple dressed in long flowing robes approached us.

"Hey, man," the bearded boy called with a sick grin through his stringy beard, "you got a fix?"

I reached in my pocket and pulled out a Gospel tract.

"The only thing that will really fix you is Jesus," I said.

He looked at me with a glassy stare.

"Where are you from?" I asked, trying to draw him into conversation.

Through his dirty beard I heard the words:

"Iowa. My old man's a fat farmer. But me and the chick here, we like it better in the Village. We can do our own thing."

He looked at the tract and scoffed: "Man, I don't need paper. I need bread. The chick needs a fix."

I started to tell him about the Bread of Life who had changed my life, but he was off, shuffling down the street. As they went by, I noticed that the girl had a chain around her neck, leading to the boy's wrist. Both had rings through their noses.

In one block on St. Mark's Place we passed nine cops,

walking in threes. We also passed five churches—all locked behind iron grates.

Gloria cringed and clung tightly to my arm as we stopped under the brightly lighted marquee of Bill Graham's Fillmore East. A flashing sign proclaimed that "The Hot Tuna" were playing inside. The line was more than a block long as kids waited to pay their $7.50 to get in.

Gloria jumped with a start as a young man sitting on the curb reached out and clutched at her foot. His eyes were glazed with dope, his beard matted.

"Hey, man, can you show me the way? I gotta find where it's all at," he said, with a vacant stare on his face.

I handed him a pocket-size New Testament.

"Jesus is the Way," I said softly. "He'll show you where it's at. He'll give you true happiness."

"Man, you gotta be crazy or somethin'," the boy said, shaking his head in bewilderment. "I ain't searchin' for happiness. I'm lookin' for a fix. I'll be happy soon as I get high again."

Waving his arm with abandon, he explained with a dazed look:

"All dudes on dope are happy. We're just a little lonely, that's all."

Lonely!

I guess if there's one word that characterizes the "now generation," it's that word, "lonely." For the last several years, since the publication of my book, *Run Baby Run,* I've been talking to kids. All over America, where I've held crusades and meetings, the kids come to me and talk. I've been in almost every state. I've spoken in hundreds of high schools and colleges. I've listened to kids in jails, juvenile detention homes, rehabilitation centers, prisons, hospitals, drug clinics, and churches. I've listened on the street corners in the ghettos and in the swankiest, richest boarding and military schools in the nation. Everywhere I go the kids tell me the same story—they're lonely.

In the early morning hours Gloria and I returned to our room. The city had grown quiet and somber, reflecting my inner mood. We closed the door of the tiny apartment where we were staying and prepared for bed. The room was quiet; only the faint honking of a horn and the occasional rattle of the elevated train sifted through the darkness. I lay in bed, barely conscious of Gloria's quiet, even breathing beside me, and stared upward, unseeing, into the night. A hundred splintered thoughts whirled through my mind. A thousand faces flashed across an imaginary screen—faces of those who had crowded the auditoriums where I had spoken, faces of children playing in the ghettos, hopeless faces reaching out with their eyes from behind bars, tearstained faces of children locked in detention homes, faces that looked pleadingly up at me from beds in drug clinics, faces filled with fear and fright. There were other faces: the faces of the boys at Outreach for Youth, the faces of my own little girls, the faces of those lonely, empty youth we had seen on the streets in East Village.

I tried to pray but the burden was too great, and my vocabulary too limited. Suddenly I found myself praying in the Spirit, agonizing, weeping, as the Holy Spirit prayed through me with words which my intellect could not understand.

I gently pushed back the sheet and slid out of bed onto my knees, still praying in the Spirit. It seemed that the burden of the world of lost youth had descended on my heart.

don't know how long I remained in that position, but

finally the burden eased. I pulled myself to my feet and walked across the room to the table where I had laid my attaché case earlier in the evening.

It was filled with unanswered letters, letters that had come in during the last several weeks from all over the nation. Letters from kids. Letters from parents. Letters from boys and girls in prison. Letters from Vietnam. Letters from the wounded youth of America. Letters saying, "Nicky, please help us."

I switched on the lamp, opened the case, and sorted through the letters. I had hoped to answer them while I was in New York. Youth write things they would never say face-to-face. They tell me things they don't dare tell anyone else, especially their parents.

I glanced at the letter on top of the stack, and then at the next one, and the next. Many of them begin simply:

Dear Nicky,
You don't know me, but I'm a fourteen-year-old boy in Detroit. I just finished reading your book and I don't have anyone to talk to. Do you mind if I talk to you?

Dear Nicky,
It's three o'clock in the morning and I don't know why I'm writing this letter except I've been up all night reading your book and if I can't pour out my heart to someone I'll explode!

Dear Nicky,
I need help. I think terrible thoughts. I know it's the drug, and I know it's killing me, but I'm hooked . . .

Dear Nicky,

I'm sixteen and I live in Dallas. I have no one to turn to. My problem is almost unbearable. I know this is a dumb letter, but please help me . . .

Most of the letters are handwritten on notebook paper. Many of them are from jails, prisons, juvenile detention homes, and reformatories. They are stamped "CENSORED" on the outside.

Dear Nicky,

I'm not sure if you're real or just made up. But I'm going to wait for a reply. I don't believe anyone is real. My folks had me put in jail when I was fourteen and I've been here for the last three years . . .

Dear Nicky,

Tomorrow morning at 8:00 a.m. I leave here, Gulfport, Mississippi, to begin a lifelong prison sentence at Porchman Mississippi Prison Farm. I killed someone . . .

Dear Nicky,

I am in the county jail for having relations with my sister. My dad caught me and broke my back with a baseball bat. After I got out of the hospital he had me put here. My sister visited me yesterday and told me Dad is trying to make out with her now. Can you help me? Can you help us?

Other letters come from the flip side of the social spectrum, such as this one from Royal Oak, Michigan:

Dear Nicky,

Even as I sit here in my carpeted room, the stereo blaring the latest Jefferson Airplane Album, I'm so miserable that I could die. My folks give me all the money I want and I spend most of it on drugs. It just gets worse and worse . . .

The daughter of a wealthy stockbroker in Delaware poured out her heart in a nine-page letter:

Dear Nicky,

I am eighteen. I made a mistake in the past and can't get it out of my mind. I am so afraid. Sometimes I think death

*would be better than living with all this. I see a psychiatrist
every week, but I'm afraid to tell him my real feelings about
things . . .*

A Jewish girl in St. Louis wrote:

Dear Nicky,
*When I was ten I burned a house down just because I
didn't like the girl who lived there. My old man bribed the
judge to let me off. When I was seventeen I was picked up by
the cops for speeding. My old man came down to the jail
drunk and mad. He hit me in the face with his fist. After he
sobered up, he sent the rabbi down to apologize for him.
Now I'm out of jail, but I'm not about to go back home. I
hate my old man, and if I get a chance, I'll burn his house
down, too. Nicky, I'm lost and I want to be found. I've let everybody down, even myself . . .*

The most tragic letters come from people so caught up in
the trap of satisfying their loneliness that they have turned to
perversion. One letter came from a teenage boy whose return
address was a midtown hotel in Denver:

Dear Nicky,
*My name is Dennis and I am a homosexual. At least, I
think I am, since I am living with an older man who tells me
he will commit suicide if I leave him. I have been studying
the Bible, trying to find what God has to say about homosexual relationships. Can you help me?*

Many letters are from young children like this eleven-
year-old schoolgirl from Boise, Idaho, who wrote saying:

Dear Nicky,

I haven't told anybody this, but my sister and I were in bed one night and I saw Mom and her boyfriend playing with each other. My dad was out of town and I started crying. I told my sister we were going to run away from home. Later my Mom's boyfriend put his hands on me, too. Now I know we're going to leave. But where can we go?

A ten-year-old boy in Ohio wrote:

Dear Nicky,

My father is a preacher, but he is a very cruel man. He preaches love, but he slaps me and my mom. If he slaps me again, I'm going to run away from home. Can I come live with you?

A letter scrawled in pencil on the back of an old sales slip came from a fifteen-year-old boy in El Dorado, Arkansas. It began:

Dear Nicky,

My name is Jim Chase and I have sinned many times and want help on how to live a better life. I am crying right now and praying that someday I can be like you and maybe God will make me happy. I'm so lonely, Nicky . . .

A sixteen-year-old girl in Nebraska wrote:

Dear Nicky,

I am filled with a cancer of hatred, distrust, and bitterness. A cancer which destroys even as it grows. I don't know "Love." My counselor says it is beyond my experience.

Nicky, I don't want to be the way I am. Please help me.
Can't you do something? I know damn well God will never
hear me. He never does. But Nicky, He's listened to you be-
fore. Maybe He'll listen again, even if it's only for me. To-
morrow I'm going to run away again, because no one cares,
no one cares, no one cares . . .

Many letters are written on the spur of the moment and
contain no return address. They are impossible to answer.
Even if I did know where to write, the answer would arrive
too late. Typical of these cries for help in the night is this
one:

Dear Nicky,
I'm writing this from a motel in Missouri. I've just left
California with my baby girl. I caught my wife in bed with
another man and couldn't stand to be there with her another
minute. She begged and pleaded with me not to leave, but I
couldn't stand the thought of ever touching her again after
she'd made love to that other guy. Now I'm halfway across
the USA and I've checked into this motel. The baby is asleep
on the bed beside me. I've been up all night reading your
book; I found it in the bookrack at the drug store. The sun is
almost ready to come up and I'm so confused I don't know
what to do. I found your address in the back of the book and
am sitting here on the edge of the bed writing. What should I
do? Should I go back? I know my wife loves me and has re-
pented of what she did. But can I accept her? I don't know
why I'm writing you, because you may never get this letter.
But I need some answers. Perhaps if I turn to God . . .

Almost every week I get a letter like this one from a seventeen-year-old girl in rural Louisiana, saying:

Dear Nicky,

I don't know who will get this letter, but I sure hope it'll be someone who will try to help me. I am so mixed up—I don't give a damn for anything. Nothing matters anymore. I am so alone that I feel empty inside—almost like I don't even have a heart. I have turned to immorality because there is no place else to turn. I am as low as a prostitute except I don't charge for the use of my body. I give it because it gives me momentary relief from my aching loneliness . . .

The same girl went on:

I just want to be me and feel free and happy at something. But I can't find it. I can't reach and catch it. Please help me. I know I'm a phony. I know I stink to God. I want to do right, but I can't. I cuss, smoke, drink, lie, steal, and shack up with any boy who is kind to me. Yet on Sunday I sing in the youth choir. My parents are too busy with their affairs to give a damn . . .

Her desperation is caught in the last paragraph of her letter:

Here I am writing to a place I've never heard of (Fresno) and to a person I've never met (Nicky Cruz). But I have got to have help. I have even considered suicide, because I don't see any other way out of it. I'm just so alone—so lonely.

She sent me several poems she had written. Like the letter, they were written with pencil on smudged notebook paper.

Somehow this particular letter and poetry seem to sum up the general feeling of so many in the present generation—the LONELY NOW.

> *Life is at its best*
> *When it's in its grave at rest . . .*
> *One day you love*
> *One day you hate*
> *One day you decide to break*
> *One day you discover your mistake*
> *But the same day you find*
> *It's too late.*
> *Life is complicated and full of sin.*
>
> *I'm so alone for love*
> *My insides cry out to God above.*
> *Oh! I need someone*
> *Whose heart I have won*
> *I am lost and lonely in this universe.*

I was startled by the soft touch of Gloria's hand on my shoulder. I could feel her body, still warm from the bed, pressed close to my back.

"Are you all right, Sweetheart?" she asked softly, her voice filled with sleep.

I reached up and took her hand with mine, the pages symbolic of hopelessness spread before me. I tried to talk, but the waves of emotion swept over my heart again, and all I could do was squeeze her hand and pull it against my face.

I felt her lean over and put her cheek gently against the top of my head.

"Nicky," she said softly, "you're just one man. You can't save the entire world. That's up to Jesus. You need some rest. It's almost dawn, and tonight you have the greatest speaking challenge in your life. Come to bed and leave all this in the hands of Jesus."

I flicked off the lamp and followed her back to the bed. Within moments her even breathing told me she was asleep again. But the images were still with me.

The common thread woven through those letters from young people was the thread of loneliness. Loneliness and fear, for they always go together. Gloria was right. I was only one man. How much can one man do? So many young people—angry at the world, angry at God, angry at authority. What could I, one person, do to help this frightened, stumbling, driven generation crying out for love?

My mind raced back to that afternoon last year in Chattanooga, Tennessee. After the Crusade meeting in the auditorium I had hurried down to the Juvenile Detention Center to speak to some of the boys on the ward. There were about thirty of them, ranging in age from eleven to sixteen. They sat obediently while I told them about Jesus Christ and His love and His deliverance. I had given an invitation and several had come forward and knelt, accepting Christ.

But I couldn't get my eyes off one little blond-headed boy sitting off to one side. He was the youngest kid there, and his oversized jail clothes seemed to swallow him up and make him seem smaller than he actually was. As the officer herded the boys together and directed them through the steel door back to their cells, the little fellow kept looking back over his shoulder, his dirty face streaked with tears.

"Sir," I called out to the officer, "do you mind if I talk to this little fellow for a moment longer?"

The officer shrugged and said, "No, you can take him in a side room if you want some privacy."

I put my arm around his small, drooping shoulders and walked with him into a tiny room where we sat on oak chairs facing each other.

"What's your name?" I asked.

"Georgie," he said, his mouth quivering.

"Tell me, Georgie, what are you doing in a place like this?"

"I ran away," he said. "Some older guys said I could go with them. We drove up from Alabama, but they left me at a filling station. Said I was too little to tag along. The cops picked me up and put me here."

"Don't you want to go back home?" I asked.

His eyes filled with tears:

"I'd rather be here than back home. That's the reason I haven't told nobody where I came from. Nobody wants me anyway. They probably don't even care I'm gone from home."

"Georgie," I said, reaching over and putting my hand on his shoulder, "do you know Jesus?"

He shook his head and the tears rolled down his cheeks.

"I-I-I don't know anybody," he stammered.

For fifteen minutes I sat there and talked to Georgie about the things Jesus had done for me. Then I asked him if he wanted Jesus to change *his* life too. He grabbed me around the waist and nodded through the tears.

"Yessir. I want Jesus to come into my heart. Will He do it if I ask Him now?"

He knelt, and while the tears flowed I listened to Georgie repent of his childlike sins and accept Jesus Christ as his Lord and Savior.

"Georgie, I've got to go now," I said. "I have to speak at

the auditorium again tonight. But I'll write you and send you some literature telling you how to walk with Jesus."

But he wouldn't turn loose.

"Please, Mr. Cruz, take me with you. Nobody here loves me. They won't care if you take me. Please take me with you."

Gently I tried to untangle his arms from my waist, but he clung tightly, desperately. The catch in my throat grew larger until I could hardly breathe. I looked upward, and it was as though I heard the voice of Jesus saying, "I didn't turn you away when you came to Me. Will you turn this little one away?"

"No, Lord," I said. "I will not turn him away."

Before I left the Detention Center, I got permission from the authorities to fly Georgie to California to Outreach for Youth. I walked with him back to the cellblock and promised him that within the week I would get the money, somewhere, to fly him to California to his new home.

As I left the cellblock, I took one last look back into the jail. My eyes fell on two more boys, both of them in their early teens, one black and one white. Their eyes were full of tears and their lips quivering as they peered through the bars. They wanted to go too.

I stepped outside into the late afternoon sunlight, leaned against the gray stone building—and cried.

Oh, God, I want to reach out and embrace all the lost kids of the world. I want to take them all home with me. But I can't. I'm just one man and our facilities are so limited and our funds are so short . . .

Oh, God, what is the answer?

I lay in bed and stared at the ceiling until the first gray of dawn lighted the wall opposite the window. A plan was forming in my mind. Even though I was only one man, perhaps I could reach out and touch the lives of countless youth through a book, a book written just to them. Once before, in *Run Baby Run,* I was able to speak to their hearts. And now there was a need to talk to young people—not about me— but about their problems. On the desk were those letters. Perhaps if I just answered them—in public, in a book—and allowed the teenagers of the world to look over my shoulder . . .

I drifted off to sleep. After lunch I would visit my old turf in Brooklyn. It had been a long time since I'd been back in Mau Mau territory. Maybe I could contact some of my former gang members and invite them to the Billy Graham Crusade. Perhaps there, in the ghetto, I would find the rest of my answer to the question, "What do the young people need most of all to meet the challenges of today?"

Little did I realize that before the sun rose on another day God would reveal—by vivid example—the answer to my question.

2

Man and the Ghetto

"Man, Nicky, you look great!"

It was China talking. After a quick lunch I had caught the subway to Brooklyn and was walking through my old turf near Washington Park. It was there I met China and Tooley, two former Mau Maus.

Tooley was pumping my hand while China ran his fingers over the lapel of my new suit.

"Where you been all these years?" Tooley asked as we stood and grinned at each other. "Somebody told me you were a preacher or something."

"That's right," I grinned, putting my arms around the shoulders of both my old friends. "I live in California and work with 'Little People,' helping them off dope."

China shook his head.

"Man, we need you right here. We got kids, eight and nine years old, shootin' heroin in the alleys. It ain't like it used to be when we just smoked pot and had a few rumbles. Things are bad now, real bad."

We stopped in a candy store and sat at a table.

"What about you guys? How's it going?" I asked.

Tooley shook his head. He hadn't changed much since I last saw him many years before. His eyes were sunk in his

face and his complexion was pale and sallow. But he was still
the same Tooley, unwilling to talk about his situation. He
changed the subject.

"Man, Nicky, I sure wish you were back here. Things just
haven't been the same since you left. You remember that
morning after we all went to St. Nicholas Arena? You led us
down to the police station to turn in our guns and our
knives."

China began to laugh.

"Man, that was wild! That cop thought we'd come to bust the joint. He couldn't believe we were turning in our weapons."

I chuckled. Those memories were still real to me, too. China looked at me.

"Hey, Nicky, how come you went off and became a preacher and me and Tooley are still here in the ghetto?"

Tooley lit a cigarette and leaned back in his chair. He began to be philosophical.

"China, me and you are losers. Nicky's a winner. But guys like you and me—we'll always be in the ghetto. We don't know nothin' *but* the ghetto and prison. I mean, man, the cards are always stacked against us. There just ain't no hope for guys like us."

"How are things *really* going, Tooley?" I persisted.

He looked up out of the top of his eyes, peering at me through his bushy eyebrows.

"You really wanna know, Nicky, I mean, like just the way it is?"

I nodded.

He shrugged.

"Not good, Nicky. Not good. I guess you know I took that murder rap for Tony. He'd already been busted by the cops three times. If they hung another one on him they'd put him away forever. Man, he had a wife and kids. Sure, he shot that bum right between the eyes, but the guy was messin' around with his wife. I was there when it happened and we all ran. But the cops caught us. I took the rap for him and spent five years in jail."

"When did you get out?" I asked.

"About three years ago. But since then I've been back twice on narco charges."

"You shootin' heroin?" I asked, looking him squarely in the eyes.

"Not now," he said frankly. "But I'm going back. Man, things are rough. Ask China."

I turned to China. He nodded and dropped his head.

"I'm twenty-eight, Nicky, and I've spent twelve of those twenty-eight years in prison. At least Tooley's got him a wife," he said. "Me, I got no one. My wife divorced me while I was in jail. This last time I was busted for five years. I never had one visitor in all that time. I never got a letter." He looked at me, wrinkling his brow as if he still found it hard to believe.

"Can you *imagine* being locked up for five years and never having a visitor—not once—and never getting a single letter? The only mail I got was when she had her lawyer send me some papers saying the divorce was final and she had taken my two kids and married some other guy."

China's dark eyes had hatred flashing through them.

"I had sworn off dope, but when that mail came I started back." His voice betrayed the hopelessness he felt in his whole being.

"But I thought you were in prison—" I said. "You didn't go back on dope *there*—"

Tooley laughed and slapped the table.

"Come off it, Nicky. You can buy dope in prison just as easy as you can on the outside. I know a lot of guys who got hooked the first time while they were in jail."

It was hard to believe. I looked at China.

"Have you seen your wife since you got out?"

He shook his head.

"Naw, but I found me a woman and moved in with her. She was about forty-five and had a couple of kids of her own.

I thought she loved me and was going to marry me. Then one night she ran out and never came back. I moved in with this other girl I'm livin' with now. She's only seventeen, but I love her and want to marry her."

Tooley spoke up.

"Hey, China, Nicky's a preacher. Why not let him marry you?"

China looked up hopefully.

"Hey, would you, Nicky? I could go get her and you could do it right now."

I grinned and pushed China back into the chair.

"It's not quite that easy," I said. "You have to have a license, blood tests, and a lot of other things. Don't rush into something that you might regret. Don't get married just because you're lonely."

"Yeah, maybe you're right," China agreed thoughtfully as he sat back down. "After all, I've only known her a couple of weeks. It wouldn't work out anyway. Nothing ever does for me."

He reached into his pocket and pulled out a crumpled pack of cigarettes. Tooley handed him his half-smoked butt and China lit his cigarette from the end. Handing it back, he sat in silence and smoked.

I turned to Tooley.

"Are you serious about going back to heroin?"

"Why not?" he shrugged, as he flicked the ash off the end of his cigarette. "Me and China just both lost our jobs. We can't get anybody to hire us because we got prison records. The parole board says if we don't work we go back to jail. So, the only thing left to do is to get someone to front for us. He'll tell the parole officer we're working for him and then we can go to work pushing dope. What else is there?"

"How did you lose your job?" I asked China.

He looked at me again, his small dark face with deep-set eyes reflecting a lifetime of hatred and bitterness.

"This girl I'm living with is a diabetic. One morning she woke up and was in insulin shock. I rushed her to the hospital and while I was waiting for the doctor I called my boss and told him I couldn't come in to work until I finished at the hospital."

China paused, his teeth clenched tight while he ground out his cigarette with a twisting kind of vengeance.

"That pig said he didn't care what was wrong with my girl; if I didn't show up for work in thirty minutes, I was fired."

China looked at me.

"Man, Nicky, I couldn't leave my girl down there all alone! She's all I got. She's the only one in all the world that loves me. How could I walk off and leave her when she needed me? A guy can get along without a lot of things, but he can't make it unless he has someone to love—and someone to love him. She ain't much of a girl, but she loves me and I love her—and we ain't got nobody else."

I looked at Tooley.

"What about you?"

He shrugged.

"I was workin' in a air-conditioning place. They said they had too many guys, so they let me go. They said they could put me back on this winter when they start workin' on furnaces. But that's half a year away! I gotta do somethin' to support my family. So . . . I'll sell dope. What else?"

I glanced at my watch.

"How would you fellows like to go with me to Shea Stadium tonight?"

Tooley brightened up.

"Are the Mets in town? I'd like to see them play."

I chuckled and said, "No, there's something a lot better than the Mets. Billy Graham's holding a Crusade."

Puzzled, China interjected, "Who's Billy Graham? And what's a Crusade?"

"Man, you must be kidding," I said in unbelief. *"Everybody* knows who Billy Graham is!"

Tooley took a final drag on his cigarette and let the smoke escape through his nose.

"Seems like I've heard of him someplace. He's some kind of a preacher, ain't he?"

I shook my head in dismay.

"He's the best-known preacher in the world. He's holding a five-day Crusade here in New York and I'm supposed to be on the platform tonight to share my testimony."

"Hey, man, let's go!" Tooley said with enthusiasm. "We ain't got nothin' else to do, and it'll give us time to be with Nicky and talk about old times with the gang."

China pushed back his chair.

"I'm ready when you are."

Dan Malachuk, my Jolly Green Giant friend, met us at the team's headquarters hotel. After supper he took us to the stadium. China and Tooley were awed by the size of the crowd that had turned out, as they put it, for a "church service." Dan took them on to the press box while I met with Dr. Graham and the team members for a time of prayer.

Moments later we were coming out of the dugout on the third-base line and marching across the field toward the platform. All around me were people, looked like forty thousand of them. On the infield, covering second base, was a huge platform. Behind the pitcher's mound was a battery of TV cameras. On a banner stretching across the centerfield fence were the words: "I am the Way, the Truth, and the Life. John 14:6."

On the platform were such celebrities as Ethel Waters and George Beverly Shea. Cliff Barrows had already finished rehearsing the choir and was seated waiting for us to take our places. Beyond the ball park I could see the lights of the Whitestone Bridge across Long Island Sound. Beyond that was the City.

I took my seat beside Bev Shea. My mind raced back twelve years when a gang of the Mau Maus had taken over a subway train and run wild through the City. We had been busted by the cops and all wound up in jail. I couldn't even speak English then. All I knew was gang rumbles, fighting, and searching for love. Now, here I was sitting on a platform in Shea Stadium, getting ready to speak before nationwide TV. It staggered my imagination just to think about it.

The service moved briskly, and before I knew it I was in front of the microphones and that vast sea of faces.

"Jesus didn't come to get man out of the ghetto," I heard myself saying. "He came to get the ghetto out of man." I was very conscious of the needs of so many as I spoke, knowing that up there in the stands were China and Tooley, and thousands of others just like them—searching for some kind of meaning in life.

Billy Graham spoke and gave the invitation—asking those who would accept Christ to come forward. Slowly at first, then, like trickling streams of water from the melting snow on a mountaintop, hearts began to thaw, and the aisles filled with people streaming forward. They formed a giant river of humanity that flooded through the gates and gathered in a huge ocean of people around the platform. I was overcome with the immensity of it all, and the tears again came to my eyes as I wept over the joy of being a part of this giant army of God.

Someone was poking me in the back. It was one of the men who had been sitting on the platform.

"Somebody wants you down there," he said, pointing to the platform steps. I looked down. There was Dan Malachuk, motioning for me. Beyond him, I could see the upturned faces of China and Tooley. They had come forward to make a decision for Christ.

The choir was still singing "Just As I Am" as I wedged my way through the mob of inquirers jammed around the base of the platform. Putting my arms around my former gang members I moved out into right field, where we knelt in the lush green grass. First China, then Tooley prayed:

"Lord, I want to be born again. I repent of my sins and take Jesus as my Savior. Tonight I die to self and make Him the Lord of my life. Please make me a new person inside."

As we were leaving the stadium China looked up. There was a new glow in his face—a glow I'd never seen there before.

"Nicky," he said with some difficulty, "you've always been our leader. We followed you to hell when you were president of the Mau Maus. Now tonight we've followed you to heaven —and that's much better—"

"That's right," Tooley broke in. "Only you ain't our leader anymore. Now we've got a new leader—right?"

I could only nod my head.

We stood for a long moment looking at the banner in center field. The stands were slowly emptying, but all around us, on the playing field, were little knots of people. Some were standing, engrossed in deep conversation as the counselors led the seekers to Jesus. Many of the young people were sitting on the grass in groups of three and four. They were engaged in intense conversations with their open Bibles on the grass between them. I glanced into the upper tier of seats on the left-field side. The section had not been used, and someone had gone through the folding seats and turned them down so the slogan, "God Lives," appeared, written in giant letters formed by the folded-down seats. Then I looked back at China and Tooley; their faces were radiant.

"That's right, boys," I could say to them now, "we *all* have a new leader. His name is Jesus."

On the way back to the hotel, China and Tooley talked without stopping. They were different persons from the ones who had gone out to the stadium just a few hours before. Instead of talking about the past, they were eager for the future.

"You know, I think I'll move out of the City," Tooley was saying. "It ain't fair to my wife and the kids to stay in the slums. Maybe I can find a small town someplace and go to work in a garage and we can start over."

China, quiet and thoughtful, mused aloud:

"I've got to get a few things worked out first. But, you know, for the first time in my life I think maybe I can make it. For the first time I feel there's someone who loves me. Jesus loves me."

I sat between them on the back seat of Dan's car while they talked exuberantly and joyfully of what the future could hold. I was lost in deep thought myself. The night before I had been praying, seeking an answer to the question: "What do young people of today need most of all to meet their problems?" Tonight, I had received the answer in the living example of Christ entering the lives of Tooley and

China. It was the same answer I had found to my own problems. It was the same answer I had been preaching all over the country. But somehow, tonight, it had come through in a different way, clearer, stronger. The answer is Jesus Christ as Lord of our lives. It's like the sign in center field said: "He *is* the way, the truth and the life . . ."

Now I'm ready, I thought, *to get to work on those letters.*

3

I'm Fifteen and Tired of Living

In my files I have a poem written by a tortured fifteen-year-old girl who on numerous occasions has tried to take her life. Her brother came to Outreach for Youth when he was only twelve years old. He stayed for two years, and during this time I had many conversations with his sister who came to visit him. They came from a broken home and both had been on drugs before they were twelve. At the age of fifteen, the girl had contracted venereal disease. Her father, a wealthy airline executive, didn't have time for either child, and the mother was too busy with her club work to care. The girl wound up in a juvenile detention center. Here is her poem, written during her fifteenth year:

> *We are the ones on whose tombs they'll inscribe*
> *Died at fifteen, buried at seventy-five.*
> *Out of the night we breathe a sigh*
> *For those who are dead, but cannot die.*

My heart breaks for kids like this, for I know what it is like to be dead spiritually and unable to die physically. You become a walking dead person, and the city becomes the land of the living dead. This girl is just one of tens of thou-

sands of youth who feel the same way. I'm enclosing portions of some of their letters which have arrived at my office. All of them are handwritten, some bear tearstains. One letter was covered with dried blood. A note on the bottom of the page explained that the writer had cut her wrists just to let me know she meant business when she said if I didn't answer her she was going to commit suicide. Here are the letters, and my answers:

Dear Nicky,

Even though I've been raised in the home of a Bible-believing minister, I've been unhappy. Most of that unhappiness was brought on by my own stupidity. I went to a couple of parties where there was smoking and drinking. Even though I didn't smoke or drink, I did tell my sister about the party. She told my dad and it was curtains for me. I've been living in prison—hell—ever since. There is no escape. I felt everyone wanted to hurt me, so at fourteen I tried to take my own life.

Allan

Dear Allan,

Your story reminds me of one that Jesus told. He told of a boy, very much like you, who thought his home was a prison also. Instead of attempting suicide, however, this boy ran away to a far country. After he got away from home, he began to realize that even though his father was a stern disciplinarian, he still loved him. The Bible says the boy "came to himself" and asked himself, "What is a child of my father doing here in this pigpen?" He arose and went back to his father, who welcomed him with a great celebration. You can read about it in the fifteenth chapter of Luke in your Bible.

I think your parents must love you very much to discipline you when you start to go wrong. True, perhaps you didn't do the things the other kids were doing, but you were there and you had no business being there. Your father, in hopes of keeping you from falling into sin, has "laid down the law."

Have you ever tried loving your father and mother? Have

you ever thought of going to them and telling them you are sorry for your rebellious attitude and asking them to show you the way? Instead of demanding your own way all the time, have you recognized that they know far more about life than you know and that they want to lead you in ways of health and happiness?

So, you think everyone wanted to hurt you. You sound like the little boy who stuck his finger in his ear and pouted:

> Nobody likes me
> Ever'body hates me
> I'm gonna go eat worms.

But suicide? That's ridiculous! God has given you a beautiful body, a good mind, and a wonderful plan for your life. To end it at the age of fourteen is nonsense. See how much God must love you? He prevented you from taking away the precious gift He had given you—your life. It seems like you would be willing to try anything before you tried suicide. Why not try His way of living, the way of love, the way of humility, the way of meekness—the way of Christ. That sounds a lot better to me than death.

Nicky

Dear Nicky,

Right now it's 4:45 a.m. and I've just finished reading Run Baby Run. *I'm sixteen and all I can see ahead of me is living, marrying, working, dying, and not much else. Is there any reason for living? No kidding, man, are we here for some real reason or is this all there is to it?*

Tom

Dear Tom,

When I was your age, I felt exactly the same way you feel. I had lost my zest for living. I had done everything, seen everything, and still was empty. The only future I could see was a continuation of the past—and I didn't think I could stand *that*. I seriously considered suicide as a way out of the ghetto—as a way out of the prison of my fear.

Then I met Jesus Christ and everything changed. I learned about the abundant life that He talks about, that He promised us. Since that day there has not been a single day when I was unhappy to be alive. Now I look forward to each new day and can hardly wait for the sun to come up, knowing that Jesus Christ has some magnificent plan for my life that very day.

The writer of Proverbs said, "A merry heart doeth good like a medicine." Enthusiasm for life is a thing of the heart. When you feel like you do, it is because your inner works are out of adjustment. I recommend you to the master fixer, Jesus Christ. He will give you a brand new heart.

Nicky

Dear Nicky,

I live in a town that has about a thousand people in it. You can't walk out the door without everybody in town knowing about it. I feel like the world is closing in on me. I need help. I'm only eighteen but sometimes I feel like fifty. I know I'm a phony—but I don't know the way out.

George

Dear George,

The only persons who are fearful of others knowing their actions are the ones who are doing wrong. If you think it's tough to live in a small town, you ought to travel with me for a month! I live in a "glass house" and the whole world knows where I am and what I am doing.

But this doesn't bother me. I rejoice in it. God knows my weaknesses and has put me in this position to strengthen me. I don't mind having the eyes of the world on me because it reminds me that I am an ambassador for Jesus Christ. And I want to be a good one. I am honored to be put in such a position of trust.

You are bothered because you think people are watching you? Hmmm!!!

Let Jesus Christ come into your heart and resurrect you. He will, you know. And then when people look at you, they won't see George at all, they'll see Christ living in you. That sounds exciting to me. I hope it will be exciting to you also.

Nicky

Dear Nicky,

Even though I'm a Christian, I've been slipping recently. This morning, during the communion service, we were singing, "Oh, how I love Jesus." And I found myself singing, "Oh, how I love Jim." Jim is this dude I make out with. Even though he brags to all his friends about how many times he's been with me, I still chase after him. I mean, Nicky, I need someone. If I can't have someone, there's no sense in living.

Lucille

Dear Lucille,

To answer your letter, I want to share another letter I received from a girl in Florida. Like yourself, she was lonely and longing for someone to fill the loneliness. She thought it had to be someone with lips she could kiss and sparkling eyes she could gaze into. Instead, she found—

Well, read the letter for yourself:

Dear Nicky,

I grew up in a Christian home and we attended church every Sunday. But inside I was tortured. There was a horrible emptiness, a loneliness that needed to be filled. I went from boy to boy, and each time I thought I had the answer; but this didn't satisfy either. Then one day I attended a prayer meeting at a home where a group of ex-hippies were testifying. They had all been on dope but now said they were high on Jesus Christ. At the close of the prayer meeting I got on my knees and they gathered around me and laid hands on my head and WOW! JESUS IS TERRIFIC!

That was six months ago and I still haven't come down. All I want to do is praise His Name. I have even been preaching on the street corners with some of the other kids in our prayer group. And do you know what, Nicky? That old longing to have some guy's arms around me all the time is gone. I mean, Jesus is the ultimate. If God wants to send me some fellow to marry one day, that's okay too. Praise the Lord for hope. But right now, I don't need anyone else—just Jesus.

Eleanor

How about it, Lucille? Are you willing to try this Jesus?

Nicky

Dear Nicky,

I'm a sophomore at the University of Minnesota. I've been having problems the last couple of years that to me are worse than anything I could dream of. I have lost all purpose in life. I find absolutely nothing to justify my existence. I hate everyone, including myself. I hate school and all it stands for. Last night I closed the garage and turned on the car motor, but my dad came out to the garage for something and got mad, saying I could kill myself doing a silly thing like that. If only he knew! If only he understood. If only he realized how desperate I am. Is there some reason for living, Nicky? Any reason at all?

Henry

Dear Henry,

You reflect the despair and boredom of so many people these days. Your letter makes no mention of God, but I counted ten "I's." The truth is that you, like so many, have become wrapped up in yourself. And this "self" can be a pretty awful cocoon.

Yes, Henry, there is reason for living. But the reason lies outside the cocoon. As long as you stay inside, you'll never find it. Come out. Come out and look at the needs of people less fortunate than you. Think of how you can help them. Look at the human suffering around you, the misery of body and soul. And then be willing to help. Say to God, "Here am I. Send me."

But you can't be sent until you have enlisted in God's army. To do this, you must repent of your selfishness and self-centeredness and be born again—just like the beautiful butterfly emerging from the cocoon. The new birth will make you free. You'll be alive to God and He will give you a whole new sense of awareness. The world will look new to you—you'll see it for the first time.

I thank God that you have come to a dead end, the end of

"self." Now you can begin to live life as it was intended to be, a wonderful, abundant life, with Christ as the center.

Nicky

Dear Nicky,

I am seventeen and I live in a foster home. I was brought up living in sin and I can't seem to get Christ in my heart. Even as a child I was always drunk or high on grass. My Mom slept with anything in pants and didn't care who she hurt. The neighbors tell me to stay away from their husbands—because Mom is a whore they think I am too.

Finally, after two years of this, I found a boy who said he loved me, and I ran away with him. When I found I was pregnant, he left me, so I came back home and told my mom. She called me filthy names. Then she and my step-dad beat up on me. He held me down while she hit me in the stomach so I would have a miscarriage. The next day my step-dad wrote me a six-page letter saying he loved me and wanted to divorce Mom and marry me so he could help raise my baby.

After I had the miscarriage, I left home and the court put me in this foster home. And Nicky, I'm so miserable. I'd rather be dead than grow up in a world like this. I know you can't answer my letter, but it helps just to get these things off my chest.

Phyllis

Dear Phyllis,

The relief you felt in expressing yourself to me can be increased a thousandfold when you pour your heart out to God. Jesus loves you with a love that is pure, selfless, and giving. He will never take advantage of you, will never condemn you, and will never accuse. All He does is love you— and forgive you.

Don't be disillusioned by the world you have seen. There's more to life than what you have experienced so far. I know. Once I was caught in the same fix. I didn't know there was anything other than the asphalt and concrete jungle where I lived in the slums. I didn't know there were green trees and fields of flowers. I didn't know there were groups of Christians who would give all and ask nothing in return. I didn't know there were people who could love me until a preacher came into the ghetto one day and said, "Nicky, Jesus loves you and I love you." I didn't know about Jesus until then, and it took a long time before I would believe it. But I believe it now. I have been set free and God has shown me that the world is full of wonderful people, born again in Jesus Christ, who really love me—and you.

Join hands with Jesus, Phyllis; join hands with Jesus Christ, the lover of your soul, and march with Him into the future.

Perhaps excerpts from three letters, all from the same sixteen-year-old girl, but written about a month apart, will help you understand just how Jesus can change your life. The first letter arrived the middle of March:

Dear Nicky,

I would like to have the faith you have, but I don't know how to get it. It's hard for me to believe. I'm sure I've sinned more than anyone else in the whole world. Can God forgive me? I have no purpose in life. Nothing seems worthwhile. I always search but never find. Nothing seems to have a purpose. I have made two serious suicide attempts and am now in a state hospital. It's hell here. I'd do anything to get out. The only thing I can think about is suicide. It's always on my mind. I can't get it off. I've cut and burned myself many

times. *Can God cure me? If you get time, please write.*
Please.

Tracy

I wrote her back immediately. Three weeks later I received
her second letter:

Dear Nicky,
Thank you so much for your letter. It really meant a lot to
me. I guess I never expected an answer. I didn't know any-
one cared that much. I've been praying, but my prayers don't
seem to go very far. I don't know if God hears. Also, I have
another problem. I hate myself. I've cut my body many times
with a razor because of it. After I cut, I pull the bandages off
and burn the sores. I can't live with me the way I am. My
body is all scarred and full of stitches. I've given my life to
Jesus, but I'm having trouble stopping the cutting.
But it is great to know that someone cares.

Tracy

In her second letter Tracy asked me if I thought it was a sin
to attempt suicide. I wrote her back saying that suicide was an
evidence of the emptiness in her life, and that God doesn't
mean for us to be empty. I told her that if she would let the
Holy Spirit come and fill her life, the desire to commit suicide would disappear.

Her third letter arrived the middle of May:

Dear Nicky,
I'm really sorry to be writing so often, but you're the only
person I can talk to. I did ask Christ into my life, and I be-
lieve He came in. I have a whole new life now. The old one

is gone. I no longer cut myself. I threw my razor blades away and the old demons no longer torment me since Jesus delivered me. I want to live now. I want to live for Him. Suicide is the last thing on my mind. There is so much I want to do! In fact, I really want to be a missionary, and only a short time ago I was cursing them for bothering me.

Tracy

So there you are, Phyllis. Tracy was much worse off than you are. And Jesus showed her the way to a new life in Him. I pray that you will find it too.

Nicky

Occasionally I will hear a preacher say, "I have faith in the youth of today." I don't. I have found that to have faith in youth—or adults, or preachers, or educators, or government leaders—is foolish. No, I have faith only in Jesus Christ, and once He comes into the life of a person, young or old, I know He will be faithful to do a good work in them. Today's youth are no worse, or no better, than the youth of any other generation. Without Christ they are lost; with Christ they are saved. When they are filled with the Holy Spirit, they can do all things through Christ who strengthens them.

I am encouraged that more and more of today's youth are "turning on" to Jesus Christ. They have been disillusioned by the phoniness and artificiality of much of the modern church. They have been driven to despair by the hypocrisy of many of their parents and adult leaders. Because of this, there has been a mad search among today's youth for reality in life. Sadly, many of them have been looking in the wrong areas—drugs, sex, violence, worldly causes. But when these same young people turn on to Jesus and receive the baptism

in the Holy Spirit, then watch out, adults! You'll be run over
by a generation of kids whose enthusiasm for spiritual things
knows no bounds.

I began this chapter with a poem from a lonely, disturbed,
searching girl. I close it with another poem, written by a
young, Spirit-filled girl who has found the Answer:

Tonight I saw my Jesus' face
His love I couldn't ignore.
I saw the eyes of peace and love
Which I'd never known before.

His face showed a deep compassion
With love I couldn't deny;
And yet His face showed justice
That made all my pride to die.

He talked with me and told me things
I'd never heard before.
It filled me with a happiness
And made my spirit soar.

I tried to share this love and peace
But no one listened to me.
Some said, "You cannot talk to God
And Him you cannot see."

I wish the Lord would show Himself
To people who can't believe.
I know He is a living Fact
For He showed Himself to me.

—Debbie Trytko
Age 17
Merritt Island, Florida

4

Fear, Frustration, and Failure

Dear Nicky,

  I am nineteen years old and work as a bookkeeper. Even though I grew up under the strict rule of my Catholic parents, I sometimes hate God. I have tried not to believe in Him, to forget Him, but I can't. He haunts me all the time. I am perpetually afraid. I hate going to sleep at night for fear that my unknown fear will invade my dreams and haunt me even there.

  I can't stand the thought of anyone loving me, because I know that once they get to know me, they will hate me as much as I hate myself.

  It's awful not to belong. I never have and never will. I don't even know why I was born. My life is an ambivalence of extreme hatred and longing for love. I'm so afraid, I know I'm going to take to the road and just keep running. I've run all my life. I never get anywhere but further imprisoned in my hatred and pride. That's the only security I know—my prison. I belong in it. I feel at home in it and know how to act. This is important to me. But I'm so alone. And scared. So very, very scared.

Carla

Dear Carla,

Your letter reminds me of the words of David so many
years ago. He said:

> Whither shall I go from thy spirit? or whither shall I flee
> from thy presence? If I ascend up into heaven, thou art
> there: if I make my bed in hell, behold thou art there. If I
> take the wings of the morning, and dwell in the uttermost
> parts of the sea; Even there shall thy hand lead me, and
> thy right hand shall hold me. If I say, Surely the darkness
> shall cover me; even the night shall be light about me . . .
> (Psalm 139:7-11)

I could not print your entire letter, but in it you mentioned that you are the oldest of thirteen brothers and sisters.
Perhaps you have felt left out, since no doubt you've had to
pitch in and do a lot of the work to help with such a large
family. Maybe you have not felt the warmth and security of
your mother and father since they have been busy with all
the other children. And so you are afraid of love from other
sources—especially from God. But God loves you anyway.
He loves you even when you are afraid of Him. He loves you
even when you don't want His love. He loves you even when
you reject Him and run from Him. And, as the Psalmist says,
you will never, never be able to hide from His love.

The Bible says that perfect love casts out fear. If you are
afraid, it is because you have rejected the love of God. It's
time to open your heart and let Jesus love you. Then you
won't need to be afraid anymore. He'll take care of you, just
as a father takes care of his family. He will deliver you from
the prison of fear and give you perfect freedom.

                                                    Nicky

Vietnam

Dear Nicky,

I was in the Bishops gang for a while and then in the Frenchmen. When everything died down around my turf, I joined the army. I'm still fighting and killing, but now instead of going to jail, I get a medal. I need your help. I want to find the happiness, peace of mind, and inner security that you have. I believe there is a God, but I don't know how to reach Him. But I know that if He helped you, He can help me too. Tell me how—

John

Dear John,

If you joined the army in order to kill legally, you joined for the wrong reason. Whenever a man kills because he wants to, or because he likes to, or because he hates his enemy—it's wrong. And this is so in Vietnam as well as in New York.

However, whether in the ghetto or on the battlefield, you can find the peace of God in your heart. I found it while I was rumbling with the Mau Maus. Others have found it while under fire in Vietnam. Once you realize that Jesus loves you and has a wonderful plan for your life, you can turn to Him and invite Him into your heart. Many people are like you, trying to reach God. But you don't have to reach for God. He is reaching for you. He loved you so much that He sent His Son Jesus to die for you. You don't have to search for Christ. All you have to do is let Him find you. Just open the door and let Him in.

Let me share a portion of a letter I received recently. It was written on a piece of lined notebook paper and was covered with smudges of mud. It came from Vietnam where it was written in a foxhole.

Dear Nicky,

   Next week I end my tour of duty here in "Nam" and will be heading home. Many of my friends have been killed over

here and most of the others around me are escaping the hell of war by smoking pot and taking drugs. But three months ago I found something that will turn me on higher than pot.

I read your book, Run Baby Run. *One of the chaplains had it and passed it around the company. The night I finished reading it, I closed the book and got down on my knees outside my tent. It was raining and I got drenched, but I looked up into the dark sky, and with the rain splattering on my iron pot and running down my face I asked Jesus Christ to take over my life.*

Kneeling there in the mud, I heard the voice of God say:

"If you want to enlist in My army, raise your hand and be sworn in."

I raised not just one hand, but both my hands, and took my oath of loyalty to Jesus Christ.

Nicky, He came into my heart that night, and for the last three months I have known such *happiness and peace. Even now I can hear the rattle of a machine gun spewing out death, but I'm safe and secure in Jesus Christ.*

I just wanted to write and say, "Hallelujah!" I'm not afraid anymore. Jesus is real to me.

Chris

I pray, John, that you will know that Jesus is real just as Chris knows—

Nicky

Dear Nicky,

I'm in prison for something I didn't do. I was with a gang of boys one evening, but I split about midnight and went home. Later the gang stopped a car in the middle of the street, beat up the man who was driving, and raped his girl. The cops rounded up the gang, including me, and the woman identified me as one of the group.

Before God, Nicky, I wasn't with them! But that didn't

*make any difference to the Judge. I don't blame the woman
—she was hysterical.*

*So now I'm serving seven to twelve years in prison for
something I didn't do. What can I do when everyone is
against me?*

Marty

Dear Marty,

The Bible tells us to avoid the very appearance of evil.
Even though you did not commit this horrible crime, your
association with the gang had branded you just the same.

Being bitter or resentful about your prison sentence can
make you become a criminal even though you were not one
when you went in. I advise you to concentrate on good behavior. You'll be free sooner that way.

But there is something more important. In the final show-
down, we answer only to God for our actions. Although you
may have to endure prison and bear the stigma of this accu-
sation the rest of your life, your conscience will be clear. I
wish you could read my mail and know of the hundreds of
people who write saying they would give their last dollar for
a clear conscience. Thank God that you are not afraid to
stand in His presence, for if you have placed your trust in
Christ, you have nothing to fear for eternity. You can depend
on the verse in the Bible that tells us that "Man looketh
upon the outward appearance, but God looketh upon the
heart." When He is for us, who can be against us?

Nicky

Dear Nicky,

*I've never written a letter like this in all my twenty-eight
years, but I'm writing to you now, a complete stranger, to ask*

*you to pray for me. Tomorrow morning at eight o'clock I
leave Gulfport, Mississippi, to begin a lifelong prison sentence at Porchman, Mississippi, Prison Farm. I am a mur-
derer, but I have accepted Jesus Christ as my personal Savior. I know Satan hates to lose a servant like me, and I'm
scared, Nicky, scared he'll pull me back down into the hell I
once knew. I just can't escape the feeling that God has a purpose for me, even in prison.*

*I know God listens to you, but sometimes I doubt if He'll
bother with me. That's why I want you to pray for me. I
have a son and daughter I'll probably never see again. All I
can do is pray that God will guide them as they go through
life without me. But if this letter can make any young person
stop and think, and hopefully turn to Jesus Christ before it is
too late, please use it, Nicky.*

Clem

Dear Clem,

I praise God you have found Jesus as your Savior. Some of
the greatest mission fields in all the world are our prisons.
Think of the opportunities you will have to witness there!

Did you know that there is one thing that man can do that
is impossible for God? That's right! Man can remember his
sins after he has been converted, but God cannot remember
them. God says, "And their sins and iniquities will I remember no more" (Hebrews 10:17). The Bible promises, "If we
confess our sins, he is faithful and just to forgive us our sins,
and to cleanse us from all unrighteousness" (I John 1:9).

Remember that you are now a Son of God. Even though
you are locked up in a prison, you do not have to fight your
battle alone. Jesus Christ, the Victor, fights for you, and He
will never let you go.

Don't sell yourself short. God will answer your prayers, just as He answers mine. God hears the prayers of every man who prays in Jesus' name. And He hears, not because we are worthy, but because He is Love.

Nicky

Dear Nicky,

I'm fifteen and I attended your Crusade in Wilmington, N.C. My life has been entirely different since then, but I'm discouraged because I still have the same urges as before. I was going pretty heavy with a boy and we decided to stop sinning after I gave my heart to Christ. Now he is asking me to start back—and I want to. What's wrong with me? Do I need to be saved again? Must I go on living such a defeated life?

Polly

Dear Polly,

God's plan for you is a victorious one. Jesus said, "I came not only to give you eternal life, but abundant life as well." Let me suggest several things that will help you.

First, your sin is forgiven. You started in a new direction when you were born again, but now you must grow. You had your sins removed when you were washed in the blood of Jesus, and now that place where they were must be filled. (Read Luke 11:24-26.)

Second, newborn infants need food regularly and in increasing amounts. We have a little baby girl in our house. Early in life she drank milk. Now she is beginning to eat baby food from a jar. As she grows bigger and cuts her teeth, she will begin to eat meat. In the same way, as a spiritual babe, you need the food of God's Word.

Third, you cannot live a life of victory without having the filling of the Holy Spirit. Jesus said:

"If ye then, being evil, know how to give good gifts unto your children: how much more shall your heavenly father give the Holy Spirit to them that ask him?" (Luke 11:13).

Be assured that God has given you victory over your temptations. The Scripture promises, "Sin shall not have dominion over you." However, if your boyfriend keeps on suggesting you fall back into sin, divorce yourself from him. I know you'll make it with Jesus.

Nicky

Dear Nicky,

I am fourteen years old and am afraid to die. Last night I dreamed a dark angel came into my room and tried to take me away into death. I woke up screaming in fear. Today I know I am not ready to die. What can I do?

Lester

Dear Lester,

God may have permitted you to have this dream to make you realize that you have neglected the most important thing in this life and the next. You can have peace in your heart and assurance of your salvation if you will humbly acknowledge yourself as a sinner, ask God's forgiveness, and trust in Christ as your Savior. Many times God speaks to me in dreams and visions, and I am thankful that He loves you enough to give you this warning.

Just ask Jesus to come into your heart. He loves you and He will take away all fear as you learn to trust Him.

Nicky

5

Straight Sex Stuff

Dear Nicky,

Drugs aren't the only thing you can get high on. You can get high on sex too. After experimenting with a bunch of fellows who just wanted to use me, I turned to God for help. But no help came. I couldn't sleep at night because I dreamed awful dreams. I spent the nights crying pitifully and praying for a change in my life. But the next afternoon I was back at those guys' apartment, letting them use me for all sorts of things. I didn't have to go back, but something kept forcing me. Is it all right for me to keep on this way?

Nancy

Dear Nancy,

No, it is not all right. You are sinning. The Bible teaches unmistakably that no fornicators or adulterers can enter the Kingdom of Heaven. No amount of rationalizing can take this fact away. The Bible says, "Flee youthful lusts," and warns against fornication.

Sex desires are perfectly normal. God Himself created this magnetism between the sexes. However, if you give yourself to lustful men, who care nothing for the real you, it is the wrong way to fulfill the sex desire. You are a person, created

50

in the image of God, and should demand that you be treated with dignity and respect.

You have tried to turn to God but the call of the world was too strong. This means you need help. Quickly, before it is too late, find a mature Christian (preferably a woman) and confide in her. Some problems cannot be handled alone, and with this one I suspect you need help. I will be praying for you.

Nicky

Dear Nicky,

My mother has told me I can go out on dates, but she has forbidden me to pet. All the kids do it, some of them even in the parking lot of our church. What's wrong with it anyway?

Sue

Dear Sue,

Petting, which is nothing more than making love without having sexual intercourse, can bring injury to the persons involved, to the conscience, and to the personality. Therefore, it is wrong.

Petting is simply yielding to the lower impulses. It paves the way for immorality.

When I began to seek a wife, I looked for a girl who had not been pawed over by some slobbering boy. I praise the Lord I found such a girl in my Gloria. One of the reasons we have had such a happy marriage is that Gloria didn't play fast and loose with her emotions and passions beforehand. Now our life is full and rich and we can enjoy the intimacies of marriage much more, because she kept herself pure and clean.

Nicky

Dear Nicky,

My parents are church members and they think I'm a good girl. I sing in the choir and work with the children in Sunday school. But during the week I can't keep my mind off a certain boy. Last week we went to his dad's cabin on the lake and spent the afternoon in sex. Now I realize I don't love him, just the sensations. I want to go back and back but I know it is wrong. I'm in the tenth grade and if my parents knew this they'd lock me in a dungeon forever.

Lois

Dear Lois,

First of all, face the fact that you have sinned. Sin needs to be forgiven. Unless it is forgiven it will lead you into more sin. Therefore, before you do anything else, confess your sin before God and ask His forgiveness.

Next, remember that Christ is stronger than Satan. Thus, I am asking you to do something specific. Go to some quiet place and kneel down and tell Jesus all about your problems. Tell Him the things you have been doing and tell Him about your temptations. Then, ask Him to forgive you and give you the power to overcome the lust which you described in your letter. Thank Him for hearing you and being your Savior and tell Him that you intend to talk to Him, anytime, day or night, when the old urges come back.

Finally, get a Bible and start reading it. Read the Gospel of John straight through. Then read it again three times. Also, turn to the Book of Proverbs in the Old Testament and read one chapter a day for the next year. That means you will have read it through twelve times in a year. Ask the Holy Spirit to interpret the passages to you, and you will find the power of God is much stronger than the power of Satan, who would pull you back to the things of the flesh. If you do this, I promise you your heart will be filled with joy and peace.

Nicky

Dear Nicky,

Last year we moved to Detroit so my daddy could go to work in a garage. My Mom works too, and I was home alone every afternoon after school until past dark. The man next door works the night shift and he started coming over. He's twice my age and has several children. One afternoon I went to bed with him and now he keeps coming back over and wanting me to do it again. I'm afraid—afraid of God, afraid of getting caught, afraid of getting pregnant. What can I do? Is it possible for God to forgive me?

Joan

Dear Joan,

The Bible teaches that before we can be forgiven we have to repent. Just being afraid you'll get caught, or being afraid you'll wind up pregnant is not good enough. You have to sincerely recognize the wrongness of adultery and realize that you have entered into a relationship which God says is to be reserved for marriage alone.

After you get things settled between you and God, you will need to get things settled next door. I suggest you tell the man that you have repented of your sin and have denounced it once and for all. Tell him that he is never to come back over to your house unless your parents are there—that you will never, never allow him to touch you again. If he persists, tell him you have no choice but to tell your father what has happened. I think that will do the trick.

Nicky

Dear Nicky,

I am a homosexual. I am living with an emotional man who is very feminine. I feel he needs me and can only function when he has someone to watch over him. If I left him he would be torn to shreds by the wolves in our society. I have been studying the Bible trying to find what God has to say about homosexual relationships. Can you help me?

Troy

Dear Troy,

Many years ago while Paul the Apostle was living in Corinth, Greece, he wrote a letter to the church at Rome. Corinth was the capital of immorality of the ancient world, giving in to homosexual practices and claiming they were of a religious nature—and therefore all right. This is what the Bible has to say about this kind of sexual perversion: "These men deliberately forfeited the truth of God and accepted a lie, paying homage and giving service to the creature instead of to the Creator, who alone is worthy to be worshiped for ever and ever, amen. God therefore handed them over to disgraceful passions. Their women exchanged the normal practices of sexual intercourse for something which is abnormal and unnatural. Similarly the men, turning from natural intercourse with women, were swept into lustful passions for one another. Men with men performed these shameful horrors, receiving, of course, in their own personalities the consequences of sexual perversity.

"Moreover, since they considered themselves too high and mighty to acknowledge God, He allowed them to become the slaves of their degenerate minds, and to perform unmentionable deeds. They became filled with wickedness, rottenness, greed and malice; their minds became steeped in envy, mur-

der, quarrelsomeness, deceitfulness and spite. They became
. . . God-haters." (Romans 1:25-30 Phillips)

My advice is to separate from this man and ask God to
help you abstain from these evil practices.

                                                    Nicky

Dear Nicky,

*I am nineteen years old and find myself drowning in a sea
of corrupt dreams. I'm overpowered by the feeling I'm homosexual and recently have found myself actually seeking
out female partners to practice with. Is there any hope for
me?*

                                                    Sharon

Dear Sharon,

By all means talk to some trusted adviser about your problem. I would suggest you consult a Christian physician or a
Spirit-filled pastor. Remember this: through the Spirit of
God you can be changed. When the Holy Spirit lives in a
person there is a great resource for power. "For God hath not
given us the spirit of fear, but of Power."

In I Corinthians 6:9 Paul talks about some homosexuals
who lived in Corinth. Then he goes on to say, "And such
were some of you," indicating that some of the homosexuals
had been changed and were now normal, happy Christians.
They had been changed by the power of God.

Some modern psychologists and psychiatrists say the homosexual is hopeless. Homosexuals themselves, enjoying their
way of life, have recently been banding together and demon-
strating in public, asking for public acceptance of their "gay"
way of life. In California, a group has even gone so far as to
form their own church. Their pastor, himself a practicing

homosexual, declares that there is no hope for the homosexual and therefore they should just "give in" and accept it. To refute this, let me share a letter I received this last year.

Dear Nicky,

I am a male Lesbian (a female who plays the role of a male in a homosexual relationship). I have been "married" four times. For six years I was caught in this kind of web, believing there was no way out. Then, through the ministry of a Spirit-filled housewife, I was delivered from the demonic grip of Satan. As with alcoholics, once a queer always a queer (but by the grace of God under control). Being a homosexual is just as much a handicap as being hooked on junk. It's a lonely and insecure life, and if anyone needs the love of Jesus Christ it is us. It's very sad to see so many of my old homosexual friends floundering about in the sea of sin, believing there is no escape. It's sad, because unless they leave the "gay life" behind them, just like the addict, they will never have inner peace. Lesbians are also God's lost sheep, and I thank God for the Shepherd, Jesus Christ, who reached out in His tender mercy and returned me to the fold of righteousness.

Lucy

The Bible tells us that faith is the substance of things hoped for, Sharon. Have faith that you can be made whole.

Nicky

Dear Nicky,

My family and I left Texas in 1958 and came to Berkeley and have been on welfare ever since. I grew up very lonely. I started running away from home, and the authorities took

*me from head doctor to head doctor. In the eleventh grade I
started drinking and running with homosexuals, but I'm still
looking for love. I've been listening to a Christian radio program and want to know if this Jesus they talk about can
really save you from a life like this.*

Rudy

Dear Rudy,

The Bible tells us that God grieves when we sin because
He loves us and desires that we be happy and have peace of
mind. The Scriptures say that all sin can be forgiven if we
turn to Jesus Christ. Jesus said to the adulteress, "Neither do
I condemn you; go your way and sin no more." Christ longs
to forgive and cleanse you, but you must accept His forgiveness.

Nicky

Dear Nicky,

*I can't keep my mind off girls. Even when I sit in class I
find myself undressing them with my eyes. At night I lay in
bed and think evil thoughts. Every chance I get I read filthy
magazines. What's wrong with me? Are all sixteen-year-old
boys like me?*

Wilbur

Dear Wilbur,

No, not all sixteen-year-old boys are like you, but some
are. Lust is the most common sex problem. Lust is desire
gone out of control. There is nothing wrong with sexual desires, but it is possible for your sexual desire to be wrongly
directed. Jesus said that the Christian must discipline his desires and so exclude thoughts of sexual relations outside

marriage. "Anyone who even looks at a woman with lust in his eye has already committed adultery with her in his heart" (Matthew 5:28).

Reading literature that is designed to be sexually stimulating is like putting garbage in your mind. Avoid it, for the mental pictures that remain will haunt you for a long time to come.

Because the sexual desire or drive, which in itself is normal, can get out of control and be misdirected, the Bible emphasizes your need for the Holy Spirit's power in your life. Read what the Apostle Paul has to say about this:

"I advise you to obey only the Holy Spirit's instructions. He will tell you where to go and what to do, and then you won't always be doing the wrong things your evil nature wants you to. For we naturally love to do evil things that are just the opposite from the things that the Holy Spirit tells us to do; and the good things we want to do when the Spirit has His way with us are just the opposite of our natural desires. These two forces within us are constantly fighting each other to win control over us and our wishes are never free from their pressures." (Gal. 5:16-17 Living Letters)

Nicky

Dear Nicky,

I really don't know how to write this, but I don't have anyone else to turn to. One of my buddies talked to his folks about this same problem and they took him to a head shrinker. Another talked to his pastor and the pastor was so shocked he called the boy's dad and there was a big fuss. You see my problem is masturbation. Something tells me it's not right. What do you say?

Roger

Dear Roger,

Although there are no bad physical effects from this selfish, lustful practice, it is a bad habit and the follower of Christ should make every effort at self-control to avoid it. The boy or girl who is unable to break this habit becomes troubled by an accusing conscience and feelings of guilt.

Continuing with this practice indicates that you are not emotionally mature. Even though the act may not physically harm the body, it does great damage to the personality. Victory over this problem can be found the same way victory over drugs is achieved—through the power of the Holy Spirit.

I am praying you will find some Christian adviser you can talk to—and pray together that God will deliver you from the habit.

Nicky

Dear Nicky,

Several months ago I made a mistake and let a boy have me. Now he's left town and I think I'm pregnant. I'm beginning my eleventh year in high school and am scared to death. Nicky, is there someplace out there in California I can come and get rid of the baby? What should I do? Please help me.

Ginny

Dear Ginny,

Go immediately to your parents and explain the entire story. They will probably be deeply hurt over what has happened, but since they love you they will stand beside you and help you in every way.

Ask your mother if she will take you to a doctor for an examination. He can tell you if you are really pregnant, and if you are, will advise you about proper care. He can also advise you concerning state-approved adoption agencies.

Also, seek spiritual help. The fact that you are in this condition is evidence of your spiritual need. Most pastors are well equipped to deal with this problem. They have had much experience in dealing with similar situations and will be able to help in seeing that the baby is well taken care of and in leading you to seek and find forgiveness through Jesus Christ.

Nicky

6

I Always Give in to Temptation

Dear Nicky,

I am twenty-eight years old and am paroled for armed robbery. I have been in and out of prison for the last eleven years. Now that I am out this time the same old urges are there. I can't help myself. Every time I see a cash register or safe I can hardly wait until I get a chance to get my fingers on it. Please help me. I always give in to temptation.

David

Dear David,

Without God no man is strong enough to resist temptation. For some the temptation is drugs. For others it is sex. Some always fall for the temptation of lying or talking about others. For many the temptation is alcohol or tobacco. Yours happens to be stealing.

God understands this. He knows temptations of this nature come from Satan. Since He knows the terrible pressures Satan keeps us all under, He sent His Son into the world—to take away the guilt and penalty of our sins and give us the strength to overcome.

The Bible says, "There hath no temptation taken you but such as is common to man; but God is faithful, who will not suffer you to be tempted above that ye are able; but will with the temptation also make a way of escape, that ye may be able to bear it" (I Cor. 10:13).

In other words, when temptations come, stop looking inward to your weakness, but turn your eyes upon Jesus. Ask God to be true to His promise and show you the way of escape.

Above all, do not deliberately put yourself in a position to be tempted, such as taking a job as a bank guard. One young person I know was delivered from drugs. The next day, rejoicing over his new freedom, he returned to the psychedelic shop to prove his strength. Before the day was over he had taken another LSD cube. Satan, whom the Bible describes as a roaring lion going about seeking whom he may devour, will tempt you at your weakest point. Therefore, do not expose your weakness to Satan's onslaughts. Do not deliberately walk into his lion's den.

One final point. The reason your heart longs to steal is that your heart is empty. Even a Christian often has an empty heart and yearns for the things of the flesh to satisfy him. The Bible says it is possible for all Christians to be "filled" with the Holy Spirit. Such an experience, if kept fresh day by day, will crowd out all the other desires. Jesus was able to resist temptation because he was filled with the Holy Spirit. Now that Jesus has returned to His father He wants to fill you with the same Spirit that occupied His body. So, after you accept Jesus and then ask the Father to fill you with the Holy Spirit, temptations can be successfully combated—not in your own power, but by the power of the Holy Spirit who fights for you.

Nicky

Dear Nicky,

I tried to commit suicide, but failed at that. I'm so confused. I know how to become a Christian but Christianity ain't my bag. Man, I need help. Right now, as soon as I finish this letter, I'm going to meet three guys in a car and we'll go through the same thing all over. I'm like putty, and all men want is to use me for half-an-hour and then push me aside. My friends tell me that if I'm going to be this way I might as well get paid for it. But you see, I'm just a foolish tenth-grade girl who is seeking help . . . but there's nobody to help me.

Laura

Dear Laura,

Let me answer you directly. First of all, I don't think you really want help. If you did, you'd be willing to try anything —even Jesus Christ. I've never known anyone who accepted Christ who wished later they hadn't. How do you know Christianity "ain't your bag" until you try it?

The fact that you recognize your problem puts you far ahead of most girls caught in this web. The majority of girls Gloria and I talk to who are misusing their bodies refuse to recognize the sinfulness of it. However, at least you know you are being "used," which is a step in the right direction.

Remember who you are. You are made in the image of God. For you, the Son of God sacrificed His life. God loves you and is close beside you. Even while you are "making out" with those boys, Jesus Christ will be right there in the car with you—loving you with a love so pure that the things of the flesh seem like filth.

Perhaps you are seeking love through illicit sex because you have never felt loved in any other way. The large number of girls that Gloria and I minister to, who are trying to break the bondage of illicit sex, tell us they were never loved as children. Thus, when they got older they tried to fill this void with counterfeit love.

Your letter indicates you have no one to talk to about this matter. Talk to God. Then seek out some understanding, mature Christian woman and talk to her. Just because a woman is over thirty doesn't mean she can't understand.

Give God a chance. He won't let you down.

Nicky

Dear Nicky,

I believe in Jesus, but am always faced with the same temptations that bugged me before I accepted Him. Is there any way to overcome these temptations?

Pat

Dear Pat,

Don't look for an easy way out. God never promised to remove temptations, but to give us the strength to overcome them. Even Jesus was subject to temptations. The Bible says "He was tested in all things like as we, yet without sin." Jesus began his earthly ministry by overcoming the temptations of Satan while he fasted in the wilderness. The night before He was crucified, some three years later, He was again subject to temptation. If Jesus had to face temptations all His life, then why should we expect preferential treatment?

Besides, temptations often have beneficial effects. "Tribulation worketh patience; And patience, experience; and experience, hope; and hope maketh not ashamed" (Romans 5:3-5). Temptation shows what people really are. It makes the Christian stronger when he, through the power of the

Holy Spirit, overcomes. It causes him to discover the resources of his power. Often during such times of temptation you will discover that Christ is real to you; you will feel the power of the Holy Spirit and will be able to rejoice over the victory. Small wonder James said, "Count it all joy when you fall into various kinds of temptations; knowing this, that the trying of your faith worketh patience. But let patience have her perfect work, that ye may be perfect and entire, wanting nothing" (James 1:2-4).

Nicky

Dear Nicky,

I am twenty-six years old and all my life I never understood God. I tried doctors, priests, nuns, and just everyday people, but no one knew the answer. I prayed to God for help, but He never seemed to answer me. It seems like I am at the crossroads of hell. Before me are wicked temptations which I know will ruin me forever, but I seem powerless to resist. Can you help me?

Dora

Dear Dora,

Let me answer your letter by sharing word-for-word a portion from another letter I received recently. It comes from a twenty-four-year-old girl in Waterbury, Connecticut:

Dear Nicky,

Last night I thought I had gone crazy. I heard a voice in my mind. I had always heard if you hear voices you've gone crazy. I asked this voice, "Who are you?" The voice answered: "I am God. I live inside every human being and I

will talk to anybody and help him, if he will only listen to Me."

So, Nicky, I started asking questions like, "Well, how come You don't do something to help all of us addicts?"

The voice replied: "I am not a heartless God. I don't make people and just turn them loose. But I also don't make people to do everything for them either. What would be the sense of that? I will take care of all problems, if you will just come to Me."

I said, "But I'm so weak. I know I can't refuse drugs."

The voice replied, "Who are you kidding? You know nothing can make you happy but Me. Next time you are tempted, come, and talk to Me and I will bring you peace."

*Even though I am a Christian I have evil thoughts con-
stantly running through my mind. I can't stop them from entering, since many of them were placed there before I became a Christian. What can I do?*

                                                    Sam

You see, Dora, your experience is not abnormal. It is Satan's
plan to distract you from Jesus by sending evil thoughts which
bother you. If I were you, I would rejoice that Satan consid-
ers you good enough to use as a target.

There is a basic difference between a Christian and a non-
Christian. When the non-Christian has evil thoughts, he
enjoys them. The Christian abhors them. Yet in the heart of
the Christian is the power, given by Christ, to select the right
rather than the wrong thoughts. Two young people walk side
by side down the street. One turns into a house where they
are having a "pot party." The other walks on to another
house where a prayer meeting is in progress. The second person was undoubtedly tempted to go with his friend to the pot
party. But as this thought came to his mind he made another
selection, and headed for the prayer meeting instead.

It is not the thoughts you have that count, but what you
decide to do with your thoughts. Some people let their
thoughts control them. Others, by the help of the Holy
Spirit, control their thoughts. One of the "fruits of the
Spirit" listed in the Bible is that of "self-control." When
Christ is your Master, then you ought to be the master of
your thoughts. When bothered by Satan, then take authority,
just as Jesus took authority over the Satanic powers when He
was on earth. Try something. The next time you find these
evil thoughts entering your mind, command in a loud voice:
"SATAN, IN THE NAME OF JESUS I COMMAND YOU

TO LEAVE MY MIND ALONE!!" If you don't think there's power in the name of Jesus, just try this the next time you're bothered, and watch Satan flee.

Nicky

Dear Nicky,

I'm in jail and am twenty years old. I have been running away just like you ran. In fact, that's why I'm here. I ran away from a county work farm and now I'm gonna go to prison. Last week a probation officer came by and prayed for me. This is the first time anyone prayed for me. He instructed me on how to ask God to come into my heart. It helped like nothing ever has before. But I'm afraid God won't stay in my heart. I know I can't leave drugs alone; yet I want to go all the way with God. I need someone to pull me out of this quicksand that I'm stuck in. I want to leave the old me behind and walk only with God. But I'm afraid. Nicky, please help me. I'm tired of running.

Joe

Dear Joe,

The Bible says if you believe on Jesus Christ and accept Him into your heart, you are saved. We must believe in Christ as our Savior at all times. That's all it takes. Salvation is not something you earn; it is something God does for you when you ask Him.

When you prayed with the probation officer and accepted Christ and His forgiveness, God forgave you. Don't doubt it, Joe. When He said He would never leave us or forsake us, He was telling the truth. Sure, we have problems and times when things seem to go wrong, but we always have someone

to talk with and help us through our bad times. That's your
wonderful Savior, Jesus Christ.

Nicky

Dear Nicky,

*I was on drugs for five years. I lived in a hippie commune
and for a time was a part of a "family" in California. Last
summer I was on the boardwalk at a Florida beach and met
some ex-hippies who were turned on to Jesus Christ. They
told me about their experiences and invited me to accept
Jesus as my Savior. I did, and since then things have been
vastly different. We preach on street corners, in parking lots,
and on the beach. But there are times when the craving for
drugs is so strong I almost die. Can you help me?*

Norman

Dear Norman,

The same Lord who changed the direction of your life can
give you victory over this appetite for drugs. You did not
mention whether you had received the baptism of the Holy
Spirit. In my work with the boys at Outreach for Youth, we
find that the appetite for drugs often remains even after salvation. Only the filling of the Holy Spirit, prayer and Bible
study can completely drive this demonic force from you.

However, don't think that the temptation means that you
are not truly converted. Such a habit has its physical as well
as spiritual effects. Drug addiction is a kind of illness, but it
was caused by your sinful desires. Now you must rely on
Christ to give you more power than the power of the habit.
This will come when He baptizes you with His Spirit. Every
day you walk with Jesus gives you more strength and power.

I urge you to pay close attention to your spiritual diet.

You can get the proper food only through a systematic study of the Bible. Sermons help. Praise helps. But nothing takes the place of a personal study of God's Word. Peter said, "As newborn babes, desire the sincere milk of the Word that ye may grow thereby." Get in a Bible-study class. If you don't have one at the house where you're staying, start one yourself. It's an absolute necessity.

Pray constantly. When the tempter comes, go to God in prayer. When you feel happy and joyful, go to God in prayer. While you are in prayer, the devil has no power. Tell God about your trouble and ask for new deliverance.

Then this final thought. When I was working with Teen Challenge in New York, we had a young heroin addict come crawling up the steps one afternoon begging for help. I ministered to him for three days. At the end of the second day he was going into convulsions as he kicked the habit cold turkey. Screaming and clawing at himself, he cried out, "If I don't have a fix, I'll die!"

My advice to him was this:

"Then die. That's what Christ is waiting for you to do so He can be the resurrection and life in your dead body."

Jesus told us to take up the cross daily and follow Him. The cross has but one meaning—death. Death to self. Death to your rights to ever have your own way. Death to the right to give in to temptation. Go ahead and die—and when you do, Jesus will resurrect you to walk in the newness of life.

Nicky

7

Does Anyone Care?

Dear Nicky,

I think you're a fake. You can't tell me that all the suffering you had in your life was changed just because one man (God) that you can't see, talk to, or touch came into your life.

I've had a life similar to yours, and I'm twenty years old and still haven't found anything like what you were talking about. If you can prove this God of yours is really what you claim, you'll have a convert. Until then, I think you're just a phony like all the rest of the folks in this stinking world.

Mack

Dear Mack,

How do you know I can't see God, talk to Him, or touch Him. Have you ever tried it? You will never know the answer until you make the leap of faith and repent of your sin and ask the "Invisible One" to take control of your life. This is more than just mouthing a few words. It is an act of desperation that says:

"Even if there is no God, I am going to turn my back on my sin and reach out in faith. Though He kill me, yet will I trust Him."

When you reach that point in your life, then you will see (as I have seen), you will hear (as I have heard), and you will be touched (as I have been touched) by the reality of the Living Christ.

God cares. He cares so much that He will wait until we cry out to Him before intervening in our lives. He cares so much He will not violate the sanctity of your freedom to reject Him. He cares enough to send His Son, Jesus Christ, to die on the cross for your sin even though you may continue to spit on Him and say it isn't so. That's how much He cares.

I can't prove that God exists by what I say. No man can. I could talk myself blue in the face and you'd never believe me. But can you deny the reality of my life? Once I was an animal in the streets of Brooklyn. I lived like an animal; I talked like an animal; I thought like an animal. Now I am a man—and it happened because Jesus Christ came into my life and changed me. You may deny everything I say, but you can't deny what has happened to me.

I think you're looking for excuses so you won't have to believe. As long as you are thinking this way, you will never see Him. However, if you change your philosophy, and start looking for reasons why you *should* believe, you'll find them all around you.

A lot of young people go through this world saying, "No one cares." That's because they don't want anyone to care. They want people to feel sorry for them. But it's a lie to say "no one cares." Jesus cares. And so do those in whom He lives. You know that if you acknowledge this, you will have to respond to His love—and that will mean letting Him change your life. Frankly, I don't think you're ready for that. When you get desperate enough to cry out to God like I did, then He will flood you with His Power and His Presence and you'll no longer be able to say you can't believe. You'll *have* to believe because He will live in your heart.

Nicky

Dear Nicky,

I'm a Puerto Rican cop in Brooklyn. Why are we put down so much? Why are there young Puerto Ricans who go about not caring and falling into their own private and secluded world of drugs? It isn't fair. All we are to the world is greasy spics. I wish I could destroy these funky, urinated tenements. I wish I could destroy the pushers and all those who take advantage of my people. But I am just one man pounding a beat, trying to enforce the law. It seems that education is the answer, but we are deprived even of this in the ghetto. Almost every day I have to arrest one of my own people who, out of desperation, had sought the only way out of the ghetto —drugs. What is the answer? Why doesn't anyone care?

Juan

Dear Juan,

Hold on a minute. I'm a Puerto Rican and I don't think the world looks on me as a greasy spic. During the last ten years I've been invited to speak in many places from the University of California to Royal Albert Hall in London. I've had Roman Catholic priests and Southern Baptist ministers come to me for advice, asking me to pray for them. Why? Not because I'm a Puerto Rican but because Jesus Christ lives in me. When Jesus Christ lives in you, people will see beyond the outward appearance and see the reality of the Living God. People in need don't care about the color or shape of the body Christ resides in. They want Jesus to speak to them.

Don't misunderstand me. I, too, weep over the miserable slum conditions in the big cities of the world. But Jesus didn't come to get man out of the ghetto—but to get the ghetto out of man. He didn't come to put a new suit of

clothes on the old man, but to put a new man in the old suit
of clothes. That's what He did for me, and that's what He
wants to do for the millions of oppressed and downtrodden
peoples of this world.

Education is only part of the answer. Jesus is the Answer.
Once a man has Jesus, he will learn. We've all seen what has
happened in the slums of the big cities. Urban renewal has
knocked down the tenement buildings and built sparkling
new apartments. Then, in less than two years, these new
apartments look like slums. The windows are knocked out,
the doors are off the hinges, children and adults alike use
the halls as toilets. You can have all the slum clearance and
education you want, but unless there is a new man in the old
body, things will be just the same as before.

Billy Graham tells of a man who took a pig and scrubbed
him clean, sprayed him with expensive perfume, polished his
hoofs, and put a pink ribbon around his neck. He took the
pig into the living room and put him on the sofa. But as soon
as the back door was open, the pig ran out and jumped in a
mud puddle. He was still a pig.

The answer to the slum problem, the answer to the dope
problem, the answer to all the social ills of the world lies
PRIMARILY in Jesus Christ. By itself, everything else is a
waste of time and money. After the people have been evan-
gelized and their lives have been changed, then the
education and urban renewal programs have their purpose.
But before anything else is done, a man must first be born
again by the Spirit of God.

                                                    Nicky

Dear Nicky,
    I am forty years old and without a single soul who loves

me. I've never written a letter to anyone in my life, but I want to know if you would send me some Scriptures here in prison that would tell me how to be happy.

                                                    Dan

Dear Dan,

The Bible does show us the way to happiness, but sometimes that happiness comes in different ways than you might expect.

I'm enclosing some Scripture verses that will point you to true happiness—which is found only in Jesus Christ. But let me quote you a few here in this letter so you can get an idea of how Jesus says happiness comes:

"How happy are the humble-minded, for the Kingdom of Heaven is theirs!

"How happy are those who know what sorrow means, for they will be given courage and comfort!

"Happy are those who claim nothing, for the whole earth will belong to them!

"Happy are those who are hungry and thirsty for goodness, for they will be fully satisfied!

"Happy are the merciful, for they will have mercy shown to them!

"Happy are the utterly sincere, for they will see God!

"Happy are those who make peace, for they will be known as the sons of God!

"Happy are those who have suffered persecution for the cause of goodness, for the Kingdom of Heaven is theirs!

"And what happiness will be yours when people blame you and ill-treat you and say all kinds of slanderous things against you for my sake! Be glad then, yes, be tremendously glad—for your reward in heaven is magnificent. They perse-

cuted the prophets before your time in exactly the same
way." (Matthew 5:3-11 Phillips)

                                                    Nicky

Dear Nicky,

*I got a letter from my wife's attorney. She is filing for di-
vorce. That's pretty rough to take when you're over here in
Vietnam trying to defend the helpless people from commu-
nism. She has taken my two baby daughters and gone off
with another man. I've tried to live for Jesus Christ, but perhaps love and faith is not all it takes to make one happy. To
her, it was money, a house, and luxury. Doesn't anyone care?
Where was God when this happened?*

                                                    Philip

Dear Philip,

A young mother, whose little boy was run down by a
drunken driver, cried out the same question you have just
asked.

"Where was God," she wept bitterly, "when my son was
killed?" A wise old preacher answered back in gentle tones,
"He was the same place He was when evil men killed His
Son."

God has not created us and left us alone. He lives with us.
He walks with us. He knows our problems and He cares. He
has sent His Holy Spirit into the world to empower men and
women to overcome problems and move on to greater things.

The reason our loved ones turn against us, the reason little
babies get run over by drunken drivers, the reason we are
nearly overcome with sickness and disease—both physical
and moral—is sin. Mankind is born in sin, and unless he is
converted and comes to Jesus Christ, he continues to live in
sin and cultivates its fruits in the vineyard of life.

It's tragic that a woman would be so heartless, cruel, and selfish that she would take the children and divorce her husband while he was overseas. I can only point you to Jesus Christ who suffered every kind of humiliation at the hands of those whom he loved—yet rose victorious over it and is alive today, giving victory to those who follow after Him.

Nicky

Dear Nicky,

I'm sixteen years old and a junior in high school. My parents are poor and because of this I can't have any nice clothes like my friends. I want to serve God but don't see how I can do it when people make fun of the way I have to dress and because we don't have a nice car like everyone else.

Sally

Dear Sally,

Jesus loves the poor in a special way and will equip you (perhaps not with money or fine clothes) to do His will. Perhaps it will be by giving you a sweet, humble spirit. Perhaps it will be by making you good, gentle, and kind. Perhaps it will be by giving you strong convictions, or maybe by giving you the special gift of love for those who are unfortunate. You should thank God that you have parents who are doing the best they can and who have taught you to love Jesus Christ and serve Him. Poverty can be a great blessing, but even if it is a handicap, I want you to know that you can rise above it and serve Christ regardless.

You're only sixteen years old, but I want to share a portion of one of the most remarkable letters I've ever received. It was written with pencil in a large, scrawled handwriting. It comes from a seventy-year-old man who lives in a railroad

shack on the Union Pacific right-of-way. He signed his name
only "Brother Nelson."

Dear Nicky,

*My soul has been galvanized by God's grace through the
tremendous inspiration I received from your testimony. I
want to smash Satan with every weapon available. I have
walked the concrete jungles of the sidewalks of New York as
far back as 1923. Please pray for me regarding my endeavors
to fast forty days for the salvation of my loved ones, especially
my dear old father who at the age of ninety-four has never
settled the old account and cannot read his title clear. I distribute Gospel literature to about forty laundromats in
Sodom and Gomorrah, better known as Las Vegas, Nevada. I
have a big problem keeping supplied. I wish I could assist
you financially but I have just a small old age pension and
before the month is half gone I am destitute. I have to sell
some of my furniture each month to buy enough gas to drive
the ten miles into Las Vegas to distribute the tracts and testa-
ments which I buy with my pension money. Many times I
walk the railroad into town and hand out the Gospel. People
ridicule me, knock me down, and push me against the sides
of the buildings. But I don't care. I'm on a mission for my
King and Praise God for strength to serve Him.*

Brother Nelson

Are you as rich as Brother Nelson, Sally? I'm sure you'll
agree that, for all his earthly "poverty," Brother Nelson has
riches in Heaven.

Nicky

8

What's All This Stuff About Jesus?

Dear Nicky,

I don't believe in God or Christ or nothing. But as of late I wonder where I'm going to. I got in trouble with the law for robbery and am on probation. I once tried to kill my Spanish teacher but couldn't do it. You were a hood once, and now you are a saint. Maybe it could happen to me, too. I put that cross on the top of the front page so God would get this letter to you. If I get no answer then I will know there ain't no God. He can't turn me down this time because I am sincere. Please write me and tell me that your book is true and what happened to you can happen to me.

Leon

Dear Leon,

The book on my life, *Run Baby Run*, is true. And what happened to me can happen to you, too. You don't have to understand it. There are many things in this world you can possess without understanding. Electricity is one of them. Few of us understand it; yet when we turn the switch the light comes on.

If you will come with the simple trusting faith of a little child and say, "Yes, Lord Jesus, I repent of my sin and accept you as my Savior," He will give you a new dimension of living. He will open up a new world that you never dreamed existed.

I don't think putting the cross on the front page of your letter helped it get to me. The cross is not a good-luck charm, rather it was the instrument on which Christ died for your sin. The Bible says, "For whosoever shall call on the name of the Lord shall be saved." This is all I did, and Christ saved me from a fate worse than death. He will do the same for you.

Nicky

Dear Nicky,

I am sixteen years old and I live in Lynn, Massachusetts. I have never been saved but I do believe very strongly that there is a God. I believe that he is a wonderful person who can help people and perform miracles. I want more than anything to be saved, but something holds me back.

Mae

Dear Mae,

In the Book of Acts, the Philippian jailer asked Paul and Silas, "What must I do to be saved?" Paul gave him a straight answer:

"Believe on the Lord Jesus Christ, and thou shalt be saved."

You are standing at the doorway of salvation. The fact that you believe there is a God and know He can save you is half the battle. The other half is accepting Him as your Savior. All you have to do is tell Jesus Christ that you are moving out of the driver's seat of your life and letting Him behind the wheel. But it's up to you to scoot over. He will not push you or force you. He's waiting for you to invite Him in.

Nicky

Dear Nicky,

   I can't accept it. I don't understand how an individual totally lacking in spiritual beliefs can suddenly have them instilled in him to such a degree that he becomes a preacher! Perhaps I have led a narrow-minded life, but I just don't believe God can do this to a person like you. It doesn't really matter, though, and you can drop this letter in the wastebasket as soon as you finish reading it.

                                  Larry

Dear Larry,

   Don't get up-tight, man! There was more to my salvation than simply one day I was a sinner and the next day I was a preacher. I needed to repent of my sinful life—which I did. I needed to turn from my evil ways and ask Jesus to come into my life—which I did. Then I had to act on my salvation, which in this case was to turn my weapons over to the police —which I did. I needed to witness to others what Jesus had done for me—and I'm still doing it.

   Remember, "Christ came not to call the righteous, but sinners unto repentance."

   A person who feels smug about his goodness never makes a good disciple of Christ. I am constantly aware of my sinful nature and am constantly asking God to keep me true. The scars of my former life are on my body. I carry a huge scar on my hand where I was stabbed by one of the enemy gangs in New York—because I became a Christian. I'm proud of that scar, but I'm not proud of the other scars, especially those I inflicted upon others while I was running with the Mau Maus in Brooklyn. But God specializes in making sinners into saints, and even though I don't understand how He did it, how His great love for me reached down from the purity

of Heaven into the filth of the ghetto and lifted me up and
put my feet on a solid rock, nevertheless I praise God for it
every day. I am constantly kneeling at the foot of the cross
and saying, with the hymn writer:

> Amazing Grace, how sweet the sound
> That saved a wretch like me.
> I once was lost but now am found,
> Was blind, but now I see.

Nicky

Dear Nicky,

At first the Lord really was in my heart. Then, all of a sudden, POW! I went wrong somewhere and it seems He left me. I've been fighting to get back to Him ever since. Please send me advice on how to get back with the Lord.

Greg

Dear Greg,

God did not leave you. You may feel that you have left
Him. And like the father in Jesus' story of the prodigal son,
He is waiting for you to return to Him.

The prophet Isaiah said:

"Seek ye the Lord while he may be found, call ye upon
him while he is near: Let the wicked forsake his way and the
unrighteous man his thoughts: and let him return unto the
Lord and he will have mercy upon him, and to our God, for
he will abundantly pardon."

Nicky

Dear Nicky,

*In my own life, I have been a Christian for some years. I
have served the Lord in various ways in the church and com-*

munity where I live. I have been successful in my profession as a doctor beyond anything I ever expected. Suddenly a few years ago, my heart and mind seemed to be turned against everything I had done with success and with the feeling of fulfillment for so long. I need help and therefore am writing you.

Dale

Dear Dale,

Jesus said that unless we become as little children we cannot enter the Kingdom of Heaven. He also said, "Take heed, and beware of greed: for a man's life consisteth not in the abundance of the things which he possesseth." Perhaps some place along the road to success you took your eyes off Jesus and began to look to material things.

I am including your letter in this book to let young people know that even though a man may become materially successful, unless he keeps Jesus first, his success does not bring fulfillment. Jesus said to the rich young ruler who, like you, had done everything humanly possible to inherit eternal life, "Sell all you have, give to the poor . . . and come, take up the cross and follow me." Later he turned to His disciples and talked about the difficulty a rich person has in entering the Kingdom of Heaven. So keep your eyes on Jesus . . . He alone satisfies.

Nicky

Dear Mr. Cruz,

I'm a career soldier here in Vietnam. I want to live for Christ, but something always seems to prevent me from making that decision. Maybe I just do not understand Him. Please help me so I can become a better man, husband, and father.

Glenn

Dear Glenn,

Last week I received a letter from another career soldier. He told of living a life of sin and debauchery while overseas. Several times he had attempted to turn to Christ, but each time his buddies in the barracks made fun of him and called him "chicken."

I want to quote one of the paragraphs from his letter:

Last Easter we had a battlefield service conducted by the chaplain. The CO made us all attend, because he knew that some of us might never come out of battle the next day. While the chaplain was preaching about the resurrection of Jesus, I got this weird feeling in my stomach. I looked around at all my buddies that I had been out in sin with the night before. I began to think, Are they going to vouch for me at the judgment? Can they give me eternal life? I began to realize what a sucker I'd been. I had let Satan fool me into thinking that I answered to my buddies, rather than to God. And, Nicky, do you know what I did? I jumped up right in the middle of the sermon and hollered at the chaplain, "Chaplain, I want to be saved—right now!" Man, it really shook him up good. But he stopped everything he was doing and told me to kneel down right where I was and ask Jesus into my heart. I did, and you know what happened? About half the other guys did the same thing. The next day some of those guys got zapped by Charlie and never came back. But it didn't make no difference anymore, because Jesus took care of them—just like He's taking care of me. Praise the Lord, Nicky! I don't have to answer to anyone but Jesus anymore.

How about it, Glenn? Is there anything strong enough to keep you from making your decision for Christ right now?

Nicky

Dear Nicky,

Me and my pa moved to Salt Lake City last year. I got picked up for runaway and forgery and bad checks. They threw me in the Utah State Memorial Hospital in Provo and I stayed there for three months on terms that if I ran away I'd go to the State Industrial School. I ran away, so the SIS is where I ended up. I'm here now, and when I get out I'm gonna turn into a Christian just like you.

Sylvester

Dear Sylvester,

Why wait until you get out? Jesus can save you right there in the Industrial School. I can't think of a finer place to witness and tell others about Jesus than where you are. When I go to a city on a Crusade I always try to visit the industrial schools and juvenile detention homes. Sometimes they won't let me in—but you're already in. Man, go ahead and accept Christ and get to work telling those other kids about how great He is.

Here's part of a letter I received from a young man in the Tucker Prison Farm, Tucker, Arkansas. He *couldn't* wait until he got out to accept Christ:

At the age of twenty-three I was six days away from my date with the electric chair. But I am thankful to God that during this time I found Christ so that when my sentence was changed from death to life imprisonment, I knew I was not only saved from death, but from the second death as well. I am still in prison, but my spirit is free through Christ. I have found that even prison can be a mission field if your heart is free in the Spirit.

You can have that experience too, Sylvester—if you're willing. God's ready.

Nicky

Dear Nicky,
I belonged to the Pagans. I was seventeen when I got out of the gang and started to work. I moved in with a girl and

she got pregnant just about the time I got busted for car theft. I've been in jail five months now. They have church people who come in here every Sunday, and I listen to them.

But they can't stay long, and I want to know how to give my heart to Jesus. Can you help me?

Arthur

Dear Arthur,

There is no doubt about God's willingness to forgive you. The Bible is filled with promises such as, "I, even I, am He that blotteth out thy transgressions for mine own sake, and will not remember thy sins."

Repentance means turning away from your sins. Make sure you have turned away from your sins. The Bible says, "Let the wicked forsake his way and the unrighteous man his thought, and let him return to the Lord . . ." You must forsake your sinful ways before you are forgiven.

When the church people come the next time, go up to the bars and talk to them. Tell them that you have repented of your sins, accepted Christ, and ask them to pray with you. Ask them if they will give you a Bible and some special literature. God's people will always respond to this kind of request, and it won't be long before you are part of some group of Christians who will be praying for you and awaiting your release from prison so you can work with them.

Nicky

Dear Nicky,

I was ten years old when I was first locked up. Now I am thirty and haven't been free but two years all this time. I have been a prisoner of Satan and a prisoner of society. I'm not asking freedom from society, but freedom from Satan and all this sin in my life—and all this hate. I want to be born again. Nicky, please answer this letter and tell me how.

Dwight

Dear Dwight,

Many years ago a man came to Jesus by night, asking how he could be set free from the prison within. Jesus told him it would be necessary to be born again. The only way you can be born again is to die first. This means you have to give up your right to hate, your right to be bitter, your right to feel sorry for yourself. All these must die. Then you must invite Jesus Christ, who is the resurrection and the life, into your dead heart. He will come in, flooding in like the sunlight enters a tomb when the doors are thrown open. He will flood you with new life—abundant life. The Bible says, "Therefore if any man be in Christ, he is a new creature: old things are passed away; behold, all things are become new."

                                                            Nicky

Dear Nicky,

I liked your book great but don't understand this business about the baptism of the Holy Spirit. My preacher says that's Pentecostal talk and I shouldn't pay any attention to it. He says ignorant kids like you in the ghetto may need stuff like that, but us good church members can get along without it.

                                                            Albert

Dear Albert,

The baptism of the Holy Spirit is a genuine experience just like salvation. It is for all Christians.

After His resurrection, Jesus took His disciples aside and breathed on them, saying, "Receive the Holy Spirit" (John 20:22). Three days after Saul (later Paul) was converted, Ananias came to him, laid hands on him, and he was "filled with the Holy Ghost" (Acts 9:17). When Paul came to Corinth he met a group of Christians and asked them, "Have ye received the Holy Ghost since ye believed?" Like your preacher, they answered that they didn't know such a thing was necessary—or even possible. The Scriptures say, "When Paul had laid hands upon them, the Holy Ghost came on them; and they spake with tongues, and prophesied" (Acts 19:6).

There are many, many other Scriptures I could quote to show you the utter necessity of every child of God receiving the filling of the Holy Spirit.

If the baptism of the Holy Spirit was essential for Jesus (Matthew 3:16-17) and was essential for the 120 followers of Jesus so they might witness (Acts 1:8, 2:1-4), then who am I to say I don't need it? As for it being reserved for "ignorant people"—that's right! "God hath chosen the foolish things of the world to confound the wise" (I Cor. 1:27). One reason so many of the modern churches are powerless is that they have trusted in their intellectual ability rather than in the Spirit of God. Yet I thank God that in these days I am seeing hundreds of our "intellectuals," including college and seminary professors, medical doctors, attorneys and judges, wealthy businessmen and brilliant scientists—all putting aside their worldly wisdom and asking God for the baptism of the Holy Spirit. One of the modern rock singers says, "Times are a-changing." He's right, for in these latter days God is pouring out His Spirit upon all flesh, just like He said He would.

Nicky

Dear Nicky,

I was saved three years ago and was "on fire" for about eight months. Now the fire has died down and I'm struggling to keep my head above water.

Ed

Dear Nicky,

Last year I won the beauty queen contest in our big high school. Now I have become a Christian and want to tell other kids about Christ, but I don't have the courage. What is the secret to witnessing?

Rhonda

Dear Nicky,

I'm a senior here at Purdue. Through the ministry of Campus Crusade I came to Christ. But still there are no bells ringing. I feel I should be telling my friends about Jesus, but there is no power inside. What is the answer?

Tim

Dear Nicky,

I've been sitting here at my desk in the guardhouse during the night shift reading Run Baby Run. Man, it really got close to me! Here in the army I keep slipping farther and farther away from God. The chapel services have no life, and the chaplains smoke and drink like the rest of us. The guys say they are "good Joes," but honestly they like to have someone down on their moral level so they won't be convicted of their rottenness. In reading your book I see where you gave up your old life (rather, He took it from you) and now you're trying to live holy, totally for God. Man, that's what I want. I want to be different. What's the secret?

Doug

I have lumped these four letters together since they talk about a common problem—powerlessness. The Christian does not have to live a powerless life. Jesus said, "Verily, verily I say unto you, He that believeth on me, the works that I do shall he do also; and greater works than these shall he do; because I go unto my Father" (John 14:12). If you believe on Jesus, you will be filled with power, and the same miracles that Jesus performed can be performed through you. However, this is impossible unless the same Spirit (the Holy Spirit) that abides in Jesus abides in you too. For it is the Spirit that works the miracles, witnesses, and gives the power to overcome temptation—not the flesh.

Jesus told His disciples who were gathered about, powerless and confused, "You shall receive POWER when the Holy Spirit has come upon you . . ." Therefore, if you want to be able to witness for Jesus, to perform miracles, to have signs and wonders following your ministry, to exercise the "gifts of the Spirit" (I Cor. 12:8-10), then you must first receive the filling of the Holy Spirit. Everything else will follow *supernaturally*.

A fellow in Vietnam found it out. He wrote:

Dear Nicky,

Last year, March 5, at 2:30 a.m., we were off the coast of Vietnam. I had been praying for the Holy Spirit but hadn't received. I looked over the port side and could see the bombs going off on the beach. I dropped to my knees on the deck and asked Jesus to set off a bomb in my heart.

Boy! Talk about "ask and receive"! Right there, holding onto the gunwale of that pitching destroyer, I was baptized in the Holy Spirit. Ever since, I have been a mainliner with the Lord. My shipmates say I'm a fanatic, because all I talk about is Jesus. But at night, a big group of the guys have been coming down to the sick bay and they have asked me to lead them in a Bible study. They want to receive the power of God too. Hallelujah! I'm high on Jesus.

Tony

9

Am I Beyond Help?

Dear Nicky,

As a child I felt unloved, rejected, scorned. I had no play-mates. Even on the crowded schoolbus I always had an empty seat beside me. Kids brushed "cooties" off if I bumped against them. I was drawn toward freaks, hippies, and other strange misfits because no one else would have me.

At the university I thought I would be accepted among my hippie friends, but it didn't work out that way. We com-peted with each other to see who was the sickest, the farthest out. I dropped my classes, quit my library job, abandoned my car in the university parking lot, and just bummed around, scavenging, panhandling, hustling. I hurt anyone that got close to me and tried suicide three times. I finally went to a minister and told him I wanted help. I told him I was afraid I was carrying a black man's baby. All he did was judge me. I grew bitter and rejected God and society. Now I am wondering—am I beyond help?

Virginia

Dear Virginia,

No, you are by no means beyond help. The very fact that you ask the question indicates that you are searching for some kind of hope in life. However, your letter shows that for years you have simply taken the path of least resistance. Like a leaf on troubled waters, you have been washed first this way and then that way by tide and wind. As a result you have wound up in a cesspool. If you are to achieve any happiness, any creativity, any usefulness in life, it will have to be because you want it more than anything.

The great people of this world who have risen above dire circumstances have first had a desire. Helen Keller, deaf, blind, and mute from infancy, rose above her handicap, with the help of a wonderful teacher, to become one of the world's greatest women. She had DESIRE planted in her. Booker T. Washington, born a slave, set his face with determination to become someone. Before he died he was acclaimed one of America's greatest black teachers and reformers, with honorary degrees from Harvard and Dartmouth.

You can reach out, even with a timid hand, and find help to turn around through the power of God. A woman dying from a hemorrhage fought her way through a pushing, shoving crowd to reach out and touch the hem of Jesus' garment. And through that touch, she was made whole. You, too, can touch the hem of His garment and be made whole. But you have to WANT to first.

Nicky

Dear Nicky,

My life has lost all its meaning. I am in my sixties and ready to give up. My parents taught me that life without Christ is meaningless, but I thumbed my nose at them and set out to do my own thing. Now, three marriages later, with children and grandchildren who hate me, I have reached the end of my way—and it's a dead end. Is it too late for me?

Mrs. B.

Dear Mrs. B.,

Your sad story reminds me of the little girl who lost her birth certificate on the way to school. Opening the door of the classroom she sobbed to her teacher, "Teacher, I've lost my excuse for being born." Perhaps you feel like this. You've never discovered the reason for living.

But it is *not* too late for your life to be changed, even though you have lived all those years without peace, hope, joy, or purpose. Indeed, the fact that you wrote me asking if I thought it was too late for you indicates that you have reached the first stage of healing: the realization that your life needs to be changed.

You say that you have reached the end of "your way." Excellent. Now turn to the One who is THE WAY. Even now God is placing His hand on your shoulder and saying, "Come unto me . . . and I will give you rest."

Although you cannot justify a wasted life, you can commit your life to Christ now and let Him turn you into a new creature. Some of the most dynamic, useful Christians I've ever known were men and women who, after having lived a life of purposelessness, gave themselves to Christ in their sunset years. You can do it too. Remember what Jesus accomplished in just three short years of ministry. If you will let His Holy Spirit guide you, then great things can happen now.

Nicky

Dear Nicky,

Nicky, will you help me? I'm a nineteen-year-old girl who started off on the wrong track in life. Now my teachers tell me it is too late for me to change—that I will be this way the rest of my life.

Louise

Dear Louise,

Your teachers are wrong! They obviously know nothing of the redeeming power of the blood of Christ. It is a great error to say, "She'll be that way the rest of her life." This is what God sent His Son, Jesus Christ, into the world for—to change people's lives. Your life is still before you and the greatest days are just ahead. I know, for once I lived in sin and knew nothing of the love of God. Then, when I was just about your age, I opened my heart to the love of Jesus and let Him take over the controls of my life. Instantly, in the blinking of an eye, He washed me clean and gave me purpose and direction in life. Many teachers, policemen, doctors, and social workers said it was too late for me. The psychologist told me I was on a one-way trip to the electric chair. But Christ changed me, and today I am as different a person from what I was then as day is different from night.

Read this letter I received from a woman twice your age who found it wasn't too late for her:

Dear Nicky,

I read your book in jail where I was being held for armed robbery. I had been a member of the Hell's Angels' motorcycle gang and later worked as a topless go-go dancer at a night club here in Los Angeles. My life was a total ruin, but after reading your book I turned to the Bible, and believe it or not, there in that prison I found Jesus Christ as my personal Savior. I was thirty-eight years old yesterday, and last night I spent New Year's Eve alone (can you imagine?) in my motel room reading my Bible and praising the Lord for my salvation. How about that? Just me and Jesus alone in a motel room. Man, it was the greatest! He's all I need!

Sylvia

Do you see, Louise? This same Jesus can enter *your* life and change it completely. Whenever you ask him.

Nicky

Dear Nicky,

I'm in jail for having relations with a minor. Last year I was here for the sale and possession of narcotics. What's wrong with me? Why do I do things like this? Just before I was busted this last time, I joined a motorcycle gang, hoping I'd find happiness there. But nothing worked. Maybe I'm just a hopeless case.

Damon

Dear Damon,

What's wrong with you is that you are without Christ. God created us to have fellowship with Him. But man chose to turn his back on God, rebel against God's plan, and live life his own way. This is the reason for all the misery in the world today. This state of living in rebellion against God's plan and purpose is called SIN. Whenever man lives in sin rather than living in righteousness, he finds his life all messed up like yours is.

But don't give up. No one is a hopeless case. Jesus Christ loves you and has died to pay the penalty for your sins. All you have to do is acknowledge Him, turn from your sin, and ask Him to come into your life and change you. When you do this, I guarantee your life will be immediately transformed and all the happiness you sought after in the things of this world will be given you, a million times over, in the joy of salvation.

Nicky

Dear Nicky,

When I was young, everyone hated us because they said my mother was insane. Later I found out she was a prostitute. Many times I came in from playing and caught her with her boyfriends. Because of this, none of the kids were allowed to play with me. I felt the whole world had deserted me. One time one of my mother's boyfriends beat me with a belt buckle because I walked into the bedroom and found them in bed. Now I'm just getting out of the girls' reformatory and want to make a new life for myself. Am I beyond help?

Ruth

Dear Ruth,

You didn't say why you had been put in the reformatory, but it makes little difference. I see that you are ready to turn over a new leaf in the book of life and start afresh. Wonderful!

No, you are not beyond help. In fact, for the first time in your life perhaps you are in the place where God *can* help you. The Psalmist said, "In the day of my trouble I will call upon thee: for thou wilt answer me" (Psalm 86:7). That's a precious promise, and I know from personal experience that it is true. I would advise you to read the entire 86th Psalm since it is the prayer of a person like us who reached out and found help from the Lord.

Forget the past. Put it out of your mind. Give your heart to Jesus Christ and ask God to fill you with the power of His Holy Spirit. Associate with Christian people as much as you can and be in constant communion with God in prayer. Your future can be bright, with Jesus.

Nicky

Dear Mr. Cruz,

I am twenty-three years old and for the last three years have been locked up in the Indiana State Reformatory on a robbery charge. I am lost, running from everything and everybody. I have no man who calls me friend. I have been ostracized by my family, and society has seen fit to put me behind bars for the rest of my natural life. If there is a God, does He have some kind of plan for me?

Jake

Dear Jake,

There is a God and His name is Jesus Christ. He does have a plan for you, a wonderful plan. Even though you may be in prison the rest of your life, your life does not have to be "natural" anymore. It can become *super*natural if you are willing to let Christ take over the controls.

While I lived in Brooklyn I was in jail many times. Since then, I have visited hundreds of jails and detention homes all over the world and spoken to prisoners about freedom, release, and liberty—all of which are available through Jesus Christ.

Here's a letter from another lifer in another prison that may help illustrate what I'm talking about:

Dear Nicky Cruz:

I have been an inmate of all the major penal institutions in Wisconsin and Minnesota. I am now serving a life sentence at the federal prison in Atlanta. While I was awaiting trial on this last charge of murder, I began to take a good look at my life. What a mess I'd made! Just as I was thinking this, I heard a voice agreeing:

"I agree, Jerry. You've really goofed your life up."

I looked up to see who had spoken, but the cell was empty. I jumped to my feet, and the voice commanded:

"Sit down. Don't get excited. It's me, Jesus. And I want to talk to you about your life. Open that Bible and begin to read."

Now, Nicky, you may think I'm crazy, but this is exactly what happened. I began to read, and the more I read, the hungrier I became to accept Christ as my Savior.

Before the day was over I had called for a preacher, and he showed me how to pray, and I got on my knees and accepted Jesus. I reversed my plea to "guilty," and am now serving life. But man, it's the greatest thing! Really! I'm not serving life, I have LIFE. I'm being used by God to preach in the

*prison and even have many invitations to preach outside of
prison. The officials let me go out in the company of a guard,
and I've spoken to thousands of people about the grace of
God behind the prison walls. Sure, I'd like to be released,
but best of all, I have been released, set free in Jesus. And if
I never get out of prison, I will stay right here and serve my
Lord with rejoicing.*

Jordan

Do you see, Jake? Maybe God is just waiting for you to open
your Bible so He can speak to you, just like He did to
Jordan—

Nicky

Dear Nicky,

*I'm twenty years old and I can't stand myself. This letter is
so stupid. I can't believe I'm writing it to a guy who may
not even exist. But who cares? I'm divorced and have a little
baby. I'm going to live with a guy who just wants to use me,
but it's better to be wanted in bed than not to be wanted at
all. I'd like to know something about the love of God that
you've experienced, but guess that kind of thing ain't meant
for the likes of me.*

Marcia

Dear Marcia,

So you've resigned yourself to a life of sin and misery.
Seeking physical love and companionship as a substitute for
the real thing, however, will lead you down a winding path
into a wilderness of great unhappiness and eventual ruin.
Jesus says, "I am the Way, the Truth, and the Life; no man
cometh to the Father but by me." If you want to know the
love of God that I am now experiencing, then you have to

seek it the way God tells you to. This is done first of all through repentance (which means genuine turning away from your old life) and faith (which means turning to Jesus Christ as your answer even though you don't understand Him).

It's never too late. Many of the letters I receive come from people in situations far more "hopeless" than yours—yet many of them have found joy and happiness and are now rising above their circumstances.

Here is a portion of one such letter. It comes from a black girl in Harlem. She is unable to read and write and had to get someone to help her with the letter:

Dear Nicky,

I'm nineteen years and have baby girl but am not marry. My friend read your book to me and after reading I don't know what happen inside me, but I cry and cry and pray at same time. The guy who hustle for me try to beat me up, but I run and hide in alley in garbage cans with baby and cry and pray some more. There in alley I gave heart Jesus and told Him I no take drugs no more. I went to small church in Brooklyn and now taken in by some Christians who help me and teach me how to raise baby for Jesus. I very happy and one day learn write so I can tell you how much Jesus mean to me.

Jeanie

This same Jesus is for you, Marcia. I pray you'll decide that you are for Him.

Nicky

10

My Parents Bug Me

Dear Nicky,

I have a seven-year-old brother and a sixteen-year-old sister. I am eleven. All three of us are adopted. Well, anyway, my problem is that I hate my mother, father, and sister. I only love my brother. I got three D's on my report card and I cry myself to sleep at night. Sometimes I try to pray like my parents said I should, but nothing comes out and I start crying again. Nothing is any fun anymore, and whenever my parents or sister talk to me I turn my head and start crying. In the summer my friend and I are planning to run away.

She hates her brother. Nicky, please, PLEASE, help me, or at least tell me someone who can. OH, NICKY, PLEASE HELP ME!

Sissy

Dear Sissy,

You don't know how lucky you are. When I was growing up in the slums of New York, I had no father or mother at all. My parents had seventeen children and had sent me from Puerto Rico to New York. I lived there for three years by myself, always running. That is what it will be like for you if you run away. You will have to keep on running.

You are very fortunate that you have parents who adopted you. Most parents just have to take what God gives them as far as children are concerned. But your parents selected you —they asked for you. They must be very special people to love you that much.

You say that they have told you to pray. You say nothing comes out but crying. Maybe there are some deep hurts down in your heart that need to be healed. Why not go to your father or mother and put your arms around them and tell them the same things you have told me? Parents who love you enough to choose you for their own daughter will surely understand. Ask them to pray for you, and to pray with you. Tell them about your fears and your hates. Don't be ashamed to tell them that you hate them, and ask their help in praying away this hate and this fear.

I myself cannot help you, but I can introduce you to someone who can. His name is Jesus Christ. Call upon Him and ask your parents to help you find Him as your personal Savior. Your life will be transformed and all your hate will turn to love.

Nicky

Dear Nicky,

My daddy is a pastor but Mom and Dad are always fighting and arguing. Most of the time it is over me. Because of this, I hate going to church and am sick of religion being forced down my throat. I hate our home and hate my parents.

Betty

Dear Betty,

I agree that your parents are setting a bad example for you. Much of the rebellion of today's teenagers comes because of the hypocrisy they see in the lives of their parents.

However, you need to remember that your parents, even though your daddy is a preacher, are just like all the rest of us—imperfect human beings. Obviously they love you or they wouldn't have differences of opinion over you. Maybe if you got your life straightened out you'd find a big change in them, too.

The fact that you wrote me after reading *Run Baby Run* means that you accept the reality of what Jesus did for me. What He did for me without parents, HE can do for you—with parents.

I doubt if your parents are trying to force religion down your throat. They see your rebellious attitude and know that unless they do something, they will soon lose you. Why don't you repent, turn from your attitudes of rebellion, and see if your parents won't change, too? Give them the benefit of the doubt. They may be nothing more than overly zealous, and in their zeal to have you discover the truth, they use the wrong methods. Perhaps they have given you opportunities they never had, so give their views prayerful consideration, and compare their teaching with the Bible. Then you will be able to make decisions of your own—with the help of God.

Nicky

Dear Nicky,

I am fifteen years old.

I am PG by my stepfather. He was drunk and came home stoned and crawled into bed with me. He beat me until he got what he wanted. Now I take a butcher knife to bed with me, but I want to use it on myself since I found out I was PG. I told my mother and she slapped my face and said I had been shacking up with some guy. I need help.

Paula

Dear Paula,

First of all let me say this: Jesus loves you. In the Psalms we find, "When my father and my mother forsake me, then the Lord will take me up." There is no need for you to think of taking your own life. It may not seem so right now, but our Lord is able to work out all things to the good of those who love Him. Turn to Jesus. Do this immediately, today. Let nothing stand in the way of your committing your life to Jesus Christ as your Master. And begin to live in His way, following all His instructions, even to forgiving those who have wronged you. Do not harbor bitterness in your heart.

Next, seek outside help. If you know a Christian doctor, go to him. Since you are only fifteen and your stepfather is the father of the child, the doctor can help make things right.

And seek help from a Christian pastor. Be frank with him and tell him the entire story. He will be able to talk with the local welfare officials and they can take action to protect you.

Above all, have faith that God will see you through. Right now I know the skies are dark and the future blacked out, but remember that God has a wonderful life planned for you. If you let Christ come into your heart as your Lord and Master, the future is as bright as the sunrise.

Nicky

Dear Nicky,

I have a super big problem. My stepfather started making love to me four years ago. When I told my mother she just laughed and said the old goat didn't have it in him. But she works at night and almost every night he comes in and forces me to do things with him. When I ran away from home my mother called the police and now they have me locked up in a girls' home where half the girls are queers. I was supposed to graduate from high school this year, but now I won't ever get out. My mother says she'll let me come home if I stop saying my stepfather does these things. Otherwise, she's going to see that I stay locked up until I'm twenty-one. What can I do?

Donna

Dear Donna,

I have called the authorities at the girls' home and talked with the headmistress. She was not aware of your problem although she does know that some of the girls in the home are homosexuals. However, now that she knows the problem, she has agreed to talk to the welfare authorities and they are going to have you placed in a foster home.

This is only half the answer, though. You have been severely emotionally damaged by the criminal actions of your stepfather. It's going to take a long time, and a lot of loving on the part of your new foster parents, to see these things through. Don't grow impatient. All the world is not like the world you've come out of. The family unit is still the basis of our society and I am praying you will find a new home where parents can love you and help you.

The most important thing is for you to accept Jesus as your Savior. "Come unto me and I will give you rest," Jesus said. Trust Him, and let Him heal the wounds and hurts of the past and give you new hope for the future.

Nicky

Dear Nicky,

I hate my house and parents. The only thing I look forward to is school because I can get "stuff" there. By stuff I mean speed, peps, grass, and other things that make life groovy.

My parents drag me to church each week. What a bore! I'm scared and don't know what to do. I want to save my money and run away. but I can't because I keep spending it on stuff.

Please help me. Please.

Nina

Dear Nina,

Church services seem boring to you because you don't identify with what is being said or sung. I felt the same way until I realized that Jesus Christ wanted to change my life. Then things got exciting. Every time I attend a worship service now, I do so with expectancy. The Risen Christ is there— and there's nothing boring about Him!

You said you wanted to save your money so you could run away. You're running away now, just as I did once. Drugs are an escape. They are for those who are too weak to face the realities of life. It takes strong people, people with backbone and guts, to look life in the face. Instead, we have a generation of weaklings who are too chicken to venture out alone without the help of chemicals. When I was president of the Mau Maus I thought I was tough. But now I realize that I was nothing but a coward, running, running—afraid to stand and face life. Now Jesus Christ stands with me, and the Holy Spirit is within me, giving me power to meet every problem and overcome every temptation.

I, too, was like you. I thought I hated my parents. But after I became a Christian a great love came welling up in my heart for my mother and father. The greatest joy in all my life was in seeing my mother come to Christ; and the saddest duty I've ever performed was returning home to Puerto Rico and preaching my father's funeral. Jesus Christ gave me this new love. He will give you love, courage, and understanding if you will invite Him into your heart.

Nicky

Dear Nicky,

My dad left home a week before Christmas. My mom chased him out, but wanted him back the minute he closed the door behind him. My dad had been seeing another woman for five years and Mom got sick of it and ordered him out. I guess wedding vows don't mean much anymore because my dad wasn't faithful and my mom wouldn't stick by him "for better or worse." Will you pray for my mom and dad? This will be hard for me to say, but will you pray for that other woman, that she may someday find God too? I figure if God can help a boy that was as lost as you once were, then He can help us.

Daisy

Dear Daisy,

It's seldom that I see the depth of maturity and love that comes from your letter. Most teenagers grow extremely bitter in circumstances like this. I thank God for your understanding, but most of all for the great love He has placed in your heart. The love you show is not a "natural" love; it could only be given to you by the Holy Spirit.

Of course I will pray for your father and mother. As for the "other woman," she, too, is one for whom Christ died. My prayers are directed for her also. It's a tragic thing when marriage vows (or any other vows, for that matter) are not taken seriously.

I hope you remember this, and when you marry, build your home on the solid rock of Jesus Christ, with both you and your husband accepting the power of the Holy Spirit into your lives to enable you to keep your vows sacred and true.

Nicky

Dear Nicky,

I am eighteen and scared of everyone. When my parents came home from vacation I found they were on the verge of separation. I couldn't believe it. They have been married twenty-five years. I lost my faith in everything. If my parents can't make a go out of life, then how can anyone?

Becky

Dear Becky,

I wish every parent could realize the almost irreparable damage done in the hearts and minds of their children in situations like this. God intended for children to look at their mothers and fathers and find earthly security—the kind of security that would make it easier for them to learn of Heaven's eternal security. It's no wonder that you have "lost your faith in everything," for the home should be the place where faith is learned.

But let me urge you to take your eyes off your imperfect parents and look to Jesus—the perfect One. Keep your eyes on Him. He will give you strength, and even more, He will give you a love for your parents and understanding of your parents' problems. I honestly think Jesus would like to use you to help them. Would you be willing? Your parents gave you life. What better way to repay their gift than to share with them the eternal life you have found through Jesus Christ? You would not be the first teenager who has led her parents to Christ and so opened up an entire new world in the home of love, joy, peace, and security. Begin to pray for them today, that they might know Him. He'll answer your prayer.

Nicky

Dear Nicky,

My dad is a preacher. I am in the sixth grade. I have problems at home and at school. My mother is a wonderful Christian but my father is a cruel man and there is always fighting in our home. My father beats me sometimes until I bleed and then tells me I need to go to the altar. I wish I had a gun so I could shoot him dead. I wish the juvenile people would come to get me.

Vance

Dear Vance,

Jesus taught us to call God "Father." But many kids in today's society cringe at the thought of God being like their daddy. I know that the Bible says, "Children obey your parents in the 'Lord, for this is right." But it also says, "And, ye fathers, provoke not your children to wrath . . ."

There is a place for punishment in the home. Much of what is wrong with our present generation is due to lack of consistent punishment for wrongs. However, when the punishment becomes cruel, it is an indication of deep psychological and emotional problems on the part of the parent.

If you will commit your young life to Jesus Christ, and let His spirit of goodness, gentleness, and self-control be in your life, then there will be no more need for punishment in the home.

Let me share with you another letter I received from a boy a little older than you. He writes:

Dear Nicky,

I am eighteen years old and was raised as a PK (Preacher's Kid). I hated having to live in the old run-down parsonage provided by the church. All my friends at school used to make fun of me, and after a while I began to hate my father because he was a preacher. It got worse when I rebelled, because if I sassed my mother or acted disrespectful toward him, he'd take off his belt and burn me good!

Last year I ran away from home and got in with a bunch of guys who were taking drugs. I listened to them talk about their parents. They called them "creeps," "weirdos," and spoke of their fathers as "the old man." I couldn't take it. Deep down inside I knew my father was a good man who loved the Lord and loved me too—even though he used to beat the daylights out of me. So I came back home. It was too late.

My father had died of a heart attack while I was out "doing my thing" and I didn't even know about it. He had

*been buried for a month when I got home. I thank God that
I know he knows I came home. And if God allows it, I want
to grow up and be just the kind of man my father was.*

Bert

Well, Vance, it's clear that Bert is looking at his "father
problem" from a slightly different perspective now that he's
grown up. Think about it.

Nicky

Dear Nicky,
*When I was eight years old I accepted Jesus as my Savior.
I am now fifteen. My parents don't believe in God, however,
and have threatened to throw me out for praying under this
roof. They will not allow me to go to any church service or
even own a Bible. Should I sneak out anyway to hear God's
Word?*

Keith

Dear Keith,
Your parents' eyes are blinded by Satan, and I hope you
will not let a single day go by without your prayers for them.
They are unreasonable in their demands, for they are refus-
ing to permit you to do the one thing that will make you a
son they can be justly proud of. Don't become discouraged
and irritated over this. Your parents need your good example. Many times children have led their parents to Christ by
letting the goodness of Jesus reflect through their own lives.
In answer to your questions, I would say that you should
take advantage of every chance you have to hear the Gospel.
Listen to it on the radio. Read your Bible, even if you have

to hide it in your room. Read good Christian literature. Perhaps you can find a teenage Bible club at school or a home prayer group in the neighborhood. In the home, be an example of a Christian by being obedient, even when your parents are unreasonable.

Nicky

Dear Nicky,

I am an eighteen-year-old Pentecostal girl. I never knew what sin was like until I read your book, Run Baby Run. *I was shocked by the immorality of the girls. It made me really appreciate my parents more, although I sometimes thought they were old-fashioned and stuffy. But for the grace of God, I could be in the same situation as those girls you mentioned in your book.*

Flossie

Dear Flossie,

Letters like yours restore my faith in the Christian home. Sometimes children think their parents are old-fashioned because they won't let them watch some of the filth on TV, refuse to let them attend dirty movies, wash their mouths out with soap if they use bad language, and apply the rod to the seat of the pants if they go against their parents' instructions. But there's nothing wrong with being old-fashioned. You might think Jesus was old-fashioned in His ideals; yet He was thoroughly modern—timeless, really—in His approach to life. I thank God for parents like yours, who, when all the world around them seems hell-bent to shake loose from the discipline of the Bible, remain strong and determined to build their home upon the solid rock of Jesus Christ. Parents like yours are easy to "honor" and "obey," and it is good that you are fulfilling the passage in Proverbs 31:28: "Her children arise up, and call her blessed; her husband also, and he praiseth her."

Nicky

11

I Am Curious—Dead

(The Dope on Dope)

Yesterday morning, before I left the house for the airport, I received three phone calls. The first call was from a divorced mother of four children. For the last year the mother has been trying to raise her children for the Lord, but the night before, her thirteen-year-old daughter had gone to a party and failed to return home. The mother was up all night, frantically calling the girl's friends and the friends' parents. None of them gave her the same story, and none wanted to become involved. The mother, fearful the child could be injured or dead, called the police.

At 9:00 a.m. the girl walked in. She admitted having taken drugs on a dare, but she didn't know where she had spent the night. The mother helped her to bed and discovered that her underclothes were missing and that the child had ugly bruises on her thighs and breasts. When the mother questioned her, the girl grew arrogant and threatened to leave if her mother didn't stop "bugging" her.

"What can I do?" the almost hysterical mother asked. "Do you know anyone who can talk some sense into my daughter?"

The second call came from the jail. An eighteen-year-old

girl, the mother of an illegitimate child, had been arrested after her father swore a warrant out against her for petty larceny. The girl admitted that while her folks were at an all-night drinking party, she and some of her hippie friends had broken into the house and had a pot party. Some of the kids in the group had stolen makeup and some other stuff from the house. The father, furious at his daughter for her immoral conduct and her refusal to give up drugs and her hippie friends, had decided to let the law deal with her. She was calling to ask if I would pay the bondsman so she could get out of jail. She promised not to "jump bond," but did say that the first thing she was going to do was to "get her old man."

I told her I could not pay her bond, but that I would try to help. I called some Christian ex-hippies in town and they agreed to go down and talk to her—straight.

The third call came from Sacramento. The father, an engineer in the space program, said that he and his wife had given up on their ten-year-old.

"He's been out every night, smoking grass and sniffing glue," he said. The father's work demanded that he be away from home a good deal and his wife was too overworked with seven other children to give special attention to this one "problem" boy.

"If you'll take him at Outreach for Youth," the father bargained, "we'll sign over full custody and pay all his expenses. But we can't handle him ourselves; he's too much for us."

Even though we are at capacity, I agreed to take him, because the father threatened to put him in the juvenile center if we could not help.

Three calls in less than thirty minutes—all involving drugs. Most of the boys who come to Outreach for Youth in Fresno have been affected by drugs.

One of the first young men to come to Outreach for Youth was an eighteen-year-old hippie named Kirk Weyant. The first twelve years of Kirk's life were spent in various foster homes. At thirteen he rejoined his biological parents in Los Angeles, although by this time he had a deep hatred for them. He ran away from home many times, living in fields, alleys, deserted buildings, or any other place he could find shelter.

Kirk joined a fast crowd and fell into a way of life that consisted of breaking into homes and stealing food and liquor—and getting drunk. By the time he was fifteen he was sniffing glue, a habit he picked up while he was in a juvenile detention center. After seeing several boys lose their minds from glue-sniffing, he graduated to smoking marijuana. He was in a detention home run by the probation department, but the boys were growing their own weed on the back side of the farm and would sneak it into the cottage late at night.

At the age of sixteen Kirk moved to hallucinatory drugs such as peyote and LSD. As he describes it, he was trying, as all hippies were, to fill the "hole of loneliness" in his heart.

Leaving the detention home, he moved to the hippie community in San Francisco known as Haight-Ashbury. Later he moved to a cave in Box Canyon in Southern California. There he dressed like an Indian and lived in tribal fashion with a large number of hippies, ranging in age from a girl thirteen to a man thirty.

Kirk's hole of loneliness seemed to grow deeper as he became more and more addicted to drugs. He had to steal for a living, snatching clothes off clotheslines, following the milkman in the early morning hours and taking the bottles from the steps, robbing stores and homes. He took more than twenty trips on LSD, used heroin and speed, and participated in the wild sex orgies stimulated by the drugs. He had seen a friend burn himself to death and was constantly just one step ahead of the police. As a result, he lost weight until he weighed only 104 pounds; he was like a crazy man.

His mother finally turned him over to a psychiatrist at UCLA, but she knew it would take more than worldly wisdom to salvage Kirk's life. Then someone told her about Outreach for Youth. One of the supervisors at the Center told Kirk over the phone, "We can help you. God has a plan for your life."

The day Kirk came to the Center, miracles started to happen. He started to have withdrawal pains. Through prayer, God healed him. He was amazed and couldn't believe all that was happening to him was real until he saw two other hippies at the Center who had accepted Jesus Christ. One of them he had known previously, and he was amazed at the change he saw in his life. One night in the chapel, Kirk accepted Jesus as his Savior also. The burden was lifted, the hole of loneliness filled, and God healed his mind.

Much of what I know about drugs I have learned from Kirk. He has remained with us at the Center and enrolled in Bible school, preparing for some phase of outreach ministry. Because I know what God can do in the lives of young men like this, I do not hesitate to tell it "like it is," to give you all the dope on dope.

Let's look at some letters:

Dear Nicky,

My name is Steve, but all my friends call me LSD. I am seventeen, and two years ago Mom kicked me out of our house and I've had a lot of trouble ever since. I live in Dallas and would like to stop the things I've been doing like you did, but I can't. Please help me before I blow my mind forever.

Steve

Dear Nicky Cruz,

Nicky, please try to help me. My parents had me put in a psycho ward because I had been sniffing glue and disobeying them. Now one of the aides in the hospital has been slipping drugs to me for doing things with him in the linen closet. I need help from someone. Will you help me . . . please . . . please . . .

Todd

Dear Nicky,

I am sixteen years old and am writing from a girls' industrial school in Birmingham. I was busted and sent here for "runaway." I used drugs, too. Sometimes I get flashbacks on

*LSD trips, even though I haven't had any in eight months.
My memories keep telling me, "When you get out of this
hole, baby, you can have all the acid you want." Something
like acid isn't easy to forget.*

Maria

In many colleges and high schools, more than fifty percent
of the students have at least experimented with drugs. The
problem is fast spreading to junior high schools, and chronic
drug use is now being reported even among elementary-
school pupils.

Drugs never satisfy. They always leave a person with the
need for "more" or "stronger" stuff. Most of the boys who
come to our house at Outreach for Youth have been on
drugs. Their testimonies are identical with those of the thousands of kids I talk to across the country, and those who write
me in the daily mail.

A boy in Durham, North Carolina, wrote:

Dear Nicky:

*I need help. I think terrible thoughts. Evil thoughts. It's
the drug I'm on. I'm hooked and can't quit. I tried to quit
last year, had a nervous breakdown, and wound up in a mental hospital. Now I'm back, taking LSD, STP, speed, and any
other junk I can get my hands on. Sometimes I mix all the
drugs together and take that—anything for a new high. I
know others are taking advantage of me because I am on
drugs and can't help myself, but I don't know what to do. I
am twenty. If I go back to the mental hospital I will commit
suicide. I can't stand it there. I need help. I know it's the
drugs, but I can't quit. Oh, Nicky, God, someone, anyone—
please help me.*

Lucas

I have studied drug addiction from the inside out. I firmly believe that Christ is the only answer in drug prevention and drug cure. Let's look at the facts, because too often what young people know about the substances with which they so glibly experiment is no more than street-corner myth and misinformation. It is not only false—but deadly. They find out the truth too late.

In this chapter I have listed the questions about drug use that I hear most often from young people. The answers are based not only on my own firsthand knowledge, but on the latest findings of the National Institute of Mental Health and other research agencies.

Is it safe to try drugs once just to see how it feels?

No! Although one-time usage may not lead to addiction, on the other hand IT MAY! Besides this, a person who wants to experiment with drugs has some serious spiritual deficiencies, or the desire wouldn't be there in the first place. The very fact that these deficiencies exist is ample warning that you won't stop with just "one dose." If smoking a marijuana joint doesn't produce the hoped-for effect, then you will probably want to try something stronger—like hashish. Then LSD. Then speed. Then heroin. And very, very few people ever start taking heroin, even one shot, without becoming addicted.

Perhaps this pathetic letter, scrawled on lined notebook paper in handwriting resembling that of an elementary-school child, will illustrate what I am talking about. The letter comes from a college graduate in Michigan:

Dear Nicky,

I have just been dismissed from the Neuropsychiatric Institute where I have been a patient for the last two months. The night I graduated from college I attended a party. Everyone was smoking grass, but I don't like the smell of the stuff. Then my boyfriend offered me a cube of LSD. I took it, but nothing happened to me, even though everyone else was nice and high. Then we drove to a guy's house, and while I was in the car it hit me.

I began to shake and sweat, and I felt like someone was pulling a band tight around my head. The whole world looked like it was a comic strip, like it was drawn by a lousy artist, and I was a cartoon character in the middle of it. I screamed, "Please help me!" When they wouldn't, I tried to walk to a phone booth to call an ambulance. But two guys tackled me and knocked me down. They said:

"You can't go to a hospital. You'll blow it for all of us."

They held me in the back seat of the car, and I felt like the top of my head was coming off. I was screaming and screamed for the next three days.

They took me to a girl friend's house. Her mother is a spiritualist who takes LSD. I was kept there for three days. My folks were frantic since I didn't show up the next day to go with them on their vacation. But these people had me locked in a back room and all I could do was scream.

At the end of the third day I got away from the house and called the police. They picked me up and took me to the hospital where I've been ever since. And all because of one lousy experiment with drugs.

Gwen

You can never be certain ahead of time as to what your own reaction to a drug experience will be. Many of the tragic happenings in the lives of drug users take place on the "first trip." More than ten percent of the people who try marijuana become chronic, compulsive users on the first experiment. Some drugs, such as LSD and methamphetamine (speed), can cause serious harm even with one experimental dosage. The risks of any kind of drug-taking are far too great for you to risk the first dose.

The young person who successfully combats the temptation to take the first drink of alcohol, or says "no" to the first offer to smoke grass or drop acid, has won a great battle in the war against Satan, who is out to destroy his life.

A sixteen-year-old girl in Wheaton, Maryland, writes:

Dear Nicky,

I've smoked pot, taken LSD, and taken many different speeds and barbiturates. But nothing seems to help. One of my friends said I should try heroin. He says he can get me all I want for nothing.

Sue

With friends like this, Sue doesn't need any enemies. Sue's friend may get her "all the heroin she wants" the first time for nothing—because Sue won't want much the first time. But three months from now, when Sue's habit has grown to fifty dollars a day, I doubt if her friend will be as generous. And six months from now, when Sue has turned to prostitution, selling her body to every crude man who's willing to pay five dollars for the pleasure of prodding her with his filthy fingers and forcing her into indescribable acts of perversion—all because she needs a hundred dollars a day to support her habit —Sue will look a long time before she finds a friend who will give it to her free. She'll know then what a sucker she's been. But it'll be too late—

A teenage boy in British Columbia, Canada, wrote:

Dear Nicky,
I have just been returned to a detention home from which
I had escaped. I have been taking pot, drugs, and hash. I
know better than to sniff glue, for that drills holes in your
brain. But the kicks I get from drugs seem to get less and
less, while my body craves more and more. This last time I
tried horse and now I'm going to have to kick cold turkey.
The desire is like a plant growing within that has to be fed
by increasing evil . . .

Charles

Addiction to drugs, whether it's psychological or physical,
is slavery indeed. A young person can become chained to a
habit with just one shot of heroin—a habit which will destroy
his life, and very probably the lives of several around him, in
a short time. And the first step to heroin addiction is smoking
pot. If you don't believe me, ask the 100,000 heroin addicts in
New York City. Nearly every one of them will tell you he
started with marijuana.

Can marijuana affect my personality?

Yes! With prolonged use it apparently contributes to se-
vere emotional problems in many individuals. If you have an
emotional problem (and nearly everyone who takes marijuana does), then this problem will not be solved, but will
be intensified and compounded by the use of the drug. Use
of marijuana often causes you to become passive and apa-
thetic, to lose your motivation and interest in activities that

once seemed important to you, and to experience memory difficulties.

Here's a letter from a young (twenty-four-year-old) mother:

Dear Nicky,

I just got out of Blue Hills Hospital in Connecticut for drug addiction. I'm trying to stay clean, but it is a long and hard fight for me. With a little help I hope to make it. I have been on drugs for nine years, most of that time just on marijuana. Only last year did I decide to look for new "kicks," and before I knew it, I was "hooked." The reason I tried stronger stuff was I felt my personality changing. After eight years of smoking grass I had become more of a vegetable than a human being. My husband had left me, saying I wasn't the same person he married. I know he was right. He smoked grass, too, but it seemed to affect him in a different way. Sometimes I would sit around the house all day, staring. He said I was like a log in bed, and finally gave up trying to love me. Yet all the time I kept puffing pot.

I thought the hard drugs would bring me out of it, but all they did was put me in so deep I had to go to the hospital. Now I'm out, and I've met Jesus Christ, and I feel His Holy Spirit transforming my personality into the personality of God. It's wonderful and I hope you'll keep on praying that I'll never, ever, be tempted to go back into the hell of nothingness caused by drugs.

Diane

God created us all with different personalities. Just as the different colors of the autumn leaves on the hillside give beauty and variety, so our different personalities give beauty to life. It's one thing to tamper with our personalties through chemicals—and quite another to let the Holy Spirit of God transform our personalities by the "renewing of our minds through Christ Jesus."

To try to change your personality through drugs is like opening the back of a precision watch and attacking it with a cold chisel. If you want a fine watch adjusted you take it to a watchmaker. If you want your personality changed or improved, then the secret is to turn it over to Jesus Christ who will set you in time with the sights and sounds of eternity.

What should I do at a party where everyone is on drugs and they're trying to get me to take them?

Leave immediately! Most people start on drugs the first time in just such circumstances. Even if you stay but don't turn on, you are in danger of being arrested. A person present where drugs are being used is guilty of breaking the law.

Isn't marijuana safer than alcohol?

Both marijuana and alcohol are intoxicants—they impair your physical coordination and hamper your judgment. In countries where alcohol is forbidden, there are skid rows created by marijuana smokers.

A thirteen-year-old marijuana smoker writes from Memphis, Tennessee:

Dear Nicky,
My old man found some roaches in my room after he and my mother came home from a drinking party. He beat me with his belt and said if he ever caught me smoking pot

again, he'd have me put in juvenile hall. What I want to know is, what's the difference between him going out and getting stoned on liquor and me sitting around the house with some of my friends smoking a few joints?

Jimmy

Dear Jimmy,

Frankly there's very little difference. Many of the over-thirty generation (including doctors and law enforcement agents who are combating drugs) see no harm in beverage alcohol. They are just as blind to the dangers, evils, and destruction of lives and property caused by beverage alcohol as the under-thirty group is to the drug problem. Don't let their blindness be a stumbling block to you. Both groups need to open their eyes to the tragedy of broken, miserable, wasted lives caused by addiction to anything less than the cause of Christ.

Nicky

Don't drugs make a person more creative?

Some drugs, such as pot and LSD, may make you FEEL more creative. But they tend to hamper your actual performance. Under drugs, your motivation to work and execute creative ideas will likely be reduced because of chemically induced lassitude and passivity.

Can I get to know myself better through LSD?

Under hallucinogenic LSD, probably the most powerful drug known to man, you may have the illusion that you are gaining great insights into your personality and behavior.

Many youth testify that LSD makes it seem as though their minds crawl out of their brains and perch on their shoulders, looking them over. This illusion takes place because notions that come to you in this highly suggestible drugged state seem much more "real" than ordinary experience. It is doubtful, however, that valid insights occur with any regularity. The psychedelic world is one of fantasy, and to the average layman it yields no more "truth" about himself than his dreams or drunken babblings.

Revelation of oneself, true revelation, comes from the Holy Spirit. God, the Creator, is the only one who knows our nature and our potential. People who have been "filled with the Holy Spirit," therefore, are capable of appropriating great gifts of wisdom, knowledge, and discernment. Gifts that come from drug use are only counterfeit, and therefore completely unreliable.

What would you do if you learned that one of your own children was taking drugs?

That, of course, is a possibility. Gloria and I have three precious children—all girls. Because I am a rather well-known preacher, my children are under more pressure than the average child. Also, the fact that I am gone from home a great deal of the time puts them under even more strain.

Gloria and I have tried very hard to instill a valid faith in the hearts of our children. We hope to lead them into a personal experience with Jesus Christ and later lead them into receiving the baptism (or filling) of the Holy Spirit. In my long experience with drug addicts, I have reached the conclusion that unless a person is filled with the Holy Spirit he simply cannot have the power to adequately resist temptation and live a victorious Christian life.

If I should discover that one of my children had been experimenting with drugs, I would handle her in much the same way as I have handled others' children caught in the same web of evil and deceit, children who have come to Outreach for Youth for help. First I would try to understand the reason why. I would look at my own life as honestly as I could and try to see where I had failed in meeting my child's spiritual needs. I would try to understand that most of our problems, parental and adolescent, stem from our striving to control our own lives and destinies, instead of allowing the Holy Spirit to control them.

I don't think I would call the police, unless there had been some violation of the law, or unless others were involved who needed police action. I would point out to my child, not just the danger of drugs, which is considerable, but the greater danger of taking her life out from under the control of the Master and letting it be open to the control of Satan. I'm not saying that the drugs are Satanic, but I am saying that they open the doors for Satan's demons to come in and take over. A life not under the absolute domination of the Holy Spirit is always open for some other spirit to come in—be it drugs, alcohol, illicit sex, selfishness, greed, etc.

Above all, I would love my child and pray for her and with her. I would go to any length, even if it meant giving up my job and moving to some distant place, to try to help her resist future temptation. For my children are my primary responsibility. A man can be a success in every area of his life, but if he fails with his own children, he is a failure.

We are starting early, while our children are still very small, to teach them about the love of God and the power of the Holy Spirit. We are teaching them about Satan and his evil ways and we are teaching them about Jesus Christ in whose Name deliverance can come to all who call on Him.

12

Let's Turn the World Upside Down

Billy Graham's New York Crusade is over. Gloria and I have
spent the last several days just relaxing before returning to
California. There we will begin packing for the fifth major
move in my life.

My moving began in 1955 when my father put me on a
plane in San Juan, Puerto Rico. I was headed for New York
City.

The second move came when I left New York to go to California
to attend Bible school. I had just been saved from the
slavery of the gang and the ghetto and it was like moving
into a new world. There I met Gloria and we were married.

The third move was back to New York with my new wife
where we worked together for two years bringing the Good
News to the old familiar neighborhoods in Brooklyn. Later
we returned to California to set up our Outreach for Youth
ministry. (All this was covered in my book, *Run Baby Run*.)

Now a group of Christian business and professional men
in North Carolina have asked me to move to Raleigh to set
up my headquarters. Although we will continue our Outreach
for Youth program, I will concentrate on traveling all
over the world speaking to youth about Jesus Christ. Gloria
and I are excited about the future.

Yet the task of trying to win the youth of the world to Jesus Christ looms like an impossible mountain before us. We know we can move it only in the power of the Holy Spirit.

Our task? Part of it is to "tell it like it is" in books. The Lord told Jeremiah "Write thee all the words that I have spoken unto thee in a book. For lo, the days come, saith the Lord, that I will bring again the captivity of my people Israel and Judah . . . and I will cause them to return to the land that I gave to their fathers, and they shall possess it" (Jeremiah 30:2-3).

I believe that prophecy today refers to the youth of the world. It is the youth, now held in the captivity of drugs, sex, and rebellion, who will one day return to the land of promise and possess it. I feel my task is to help bring them to the point of commitment so they can achieve this virtually impossible task.

These are "latter days," and it is warned in the Bible that not only will the Spirit of God be poured out on all flesh, but Satan, like a roaring lion, will prowl the streets of the cities, the sidewalks of the villages, even the rural areas of the world —to seek whom he may devour. While some youth are "turning on" to Jesus, the countless majority are seeking their identity in the slavery of dope and rebellion.

Late this afternoon we drove down to the Eastside Airline Terminal to pick up my tickets. I came back outside and waited for Gloria to circle the block and pick me up. Across the street there is a small park. It's a lonely patch of struggling green and hard-packed sand cowering between skyscraper apartments, office buildings, and dirty factories belching filthy smoke into the polluted air of the city. Inside the steel-grated enclosure of the park, a few children splashed in a concrete wading pool and clambered through monkey bars.

Bored parents sat and waited, sipping warm beer and reading the paper.

I could not get my eyes off the two shabby men who sat on a green park bench facing the litter-covered street. They were thin and emaciated, both scraggly-bearded and ageless. They could have been nineteen or ninety. The ravages of drugs had taken their toll. They were a part of the horde of more than 100,000 heroin addicts who walk the streets of New York like zombies. Their shirts and pants were ill-fitting, stained with food, vomit, and urine. Both were glazed-eyed and shaking, too weak to even get up and panhandle.

The man nearest me bent forward, his head almost between his knees. His filthy once-blond beard was matted, his hair stringy. As I got closer I could see the open, running sores on his scalp where his hair had fallen out. Like the skin of many addicts whose metabolism is low, his skin refused to heal once it was broken. The scratches had abscessed, leaving gaping raw spots. Perhaps, like many junkies, he was also filled with a venereal disease.

He heaved, time and time again. A small puddle formed at his feet. Now he was empty. Dry. But the heaving continued. Soon he would heave blood.

Every fibre in his body cried out for a "fix." But heroin is up to seven dollars for just barely enough of the white powder to cover the bottom of a bottle cap which would serve as a "cooker" for the powder mixed with water and heated over a match. His arms were a mass of scars where countless needles, pins, even nails had been used to open the veins so he could "mainline" the drug.

His partner, nose running down over his lips and into his stubby gray beard, was oblivious of his companion's misery. His eyes were dilated like black holes in his bony skull.

A young man approached. Late teens. Pale blue eyes sunk deep in their sockets. Sallow skin pulled taut over his cheekbones. His nose, too, was running, and he shuffled as he walked, hands stuck deep in the empty pockets of his baggy, stained pants. His filthy tennis shoes had large holes worn on the tops and sides. He wore no socks or belt and had no shirt under his flimsy, torn jacket. His hair hung long down the back of his neck.

Graybeard on the bench lifted his eyes as he walked up. His face was expressionless, his voice flat. "You made your expenses yet today?"

"Not yet; I need forty more."

"Got any ideas."

"Don't make no difference, man. I gotta get it or die."

He nodded at the other man who rocked on the bench, head between his knees, moaning loudly. "What about him?"

"Rough, man. He's been six hours without a fix."

The younger man shook his head, wiped his nose on the back of his hand, sniffed, and shuffled off.

The honking of the car behind me told me Gloria had returned. She slipped over as I slid beneath the wheel. Moments later we were back in the traffic, heading for a Manhattan restaurant where we were to meet friends for dinner.

Gloria sensed my anguish. "What's the matter, Nicky?"

I told her briefly what I had just seen.

"But Nicky, New York's full of that. Why should you get so upset over a few junkies?"

I couldn't explain, but my spirit was in the depths of depression. Just seeing them there . . . so hopeless . . . so lonely . . . like walking dead men. Perhaps it was because I had seen the great victory Jesus had won with China and

Tooley and yet was now reminded that for every one saved, there are a hundred others still lost.

"Nicky," Gloria said as we drove through the heavy traffic, "maybe God let you take that last glimpse at the way things really are to remind you that you can never, never give up the battle. Somebody's got to turn this world upside down, and only Jesus can do it. But if He doesn't have you to stay out there on the firing line, then the battle may be lost."

I nodded my head in silence. There's always a tendency, after you taste victory, to let down your defenses. But God was showing me the problem is too big for me to ever slow down, much less retreat. More youth died from heroin usage over the last ten years than were killed in the war in Vietnam. Last year more than 900 persons died from overdoses of heroin in New York City alone. More than twenty-five percent of these were eighteen or younger. In the City today, more deaths can be traced to the use of heroin than to any other factor among people between the ages of eighteen and thirty-five—including automobile accidents and disease.

Weaving through the noisy traffic, we turned left on the Avenue of the Americas. My mind flashed back to yesterday afternoon when I had spent several hours in Spanish Harlem. There, walking down the streets, I looked up at the windows covered with the gray mesh screens. The streets were crowded with children who lived in the cramped, filthy slums. They were bouncing balls off the walls and chasing each other through the traffic. I stepped on a discarded beer can and almost fell.

I saw little kids in the basements of the apartment slums —shooting heroin with needles. Some of them had already picked up a $25-a-day habit. Where does an eleven-year-old kid get $25 a day? The same place his eighteen-year-old brother gets his $100-a-day expenses: he steals it or he sells drugs to earn it. Or, if he's enterprising enough, he may hustle and pimp on the streets for his sister or mother—and they let him have a percentage of the amount of business he can pull in.

We parked the car in a parking garage and walked toward the restaurant. I had lost my appetite, however. I could understand Jesus' answer to His disciples who urged him to eat: "I have food to eat of which you know nothing . . . It is meat and drink for me to do the will of Him who sent me until I have finished his work . . . Look on the fields; they are already white, ripe for harvest" (John 4:32, 34-35).

During dinner I could think of nothing but the heroin jungle outside the restaurant. I remembered the guys who came out of prison and couldn't get jobs, so they worked for a few dollars a week to appease the parole officer—and stole to make a living.

I remembered China's words: "A guy can kick the habit if he has someone who loves him . . . someone to love. Having someone who cares makes life worth living."

I remembered Tooley saying, "I wish the neighborhood was like it used to be, Nicky. Back then we had the security of the gang. Now the gangs are broken up and everyone is doing his own thing—with drugs. Even the little kids, ten and eleven years old, are mainlining—especially the girls. The pimps start them early so they can use them for prostitutes. By the time they're twenty they're burned out, so they have to keep getting the young girls hooked so they can earn them a living."

After dinner we walked through Times Square. New York,

once called the melting pot of the world, has degenerated
into a cesspool of drugs and pornography. From almost every
window—and from every theatre billboard—huge pictures of
nude men and women beckoned for attention and money.
The sidewalks were jammed with drug addicts, prostitutes,
and sexual perverts—all buying and selling. I shuddered
and drew Gloria close to me. *Except for the grace of God*, I
thought . . .

It is 1:00 a.m. as I sit at this tiny table writing. Tomorrow
we will be on a jet heading back to California, but before
me are these scattered papers, and in my mind are the memories of today which are burning a hole in my soul like a
blowtorch pointed at a silk curtain.

China said, "Having someone who cares makes life worth
living. Without someone to love, and someone who loves you,
there's no reason for being here."

He's right. But the answer is not in "flesh and blood" com-
panionships. It is in the presence and person of Jesus Christ.
Yet it seems that the image of Christ is distorted even by
those who are supposed to present Him.

I glance at a letter which I had answered. It was from a
schoolteacher in Clarksburg, West Virginia.

Dear Nicky:

*We live in a small city, but our problems are getting bigger
every day. Drugs are the concern of all of us. It has recently
affected me because my own daughter tried some. A lot of
the kids at school are using and selling drugs. The ministers
of the city have tried everything they know to help, but nothing works. They have had electric masses, youth rallies, and*

youth conventions. There is something missing in all these
meetings. Does the religion of today have the answers?

Serena

I wrote her back saying:

Dear Serena:

No, the religion of today does not have the answers. The
only answer lies in the religion of the New Testament, and
that means a personal, direct confrontation with Jesus Christ.
Most "religions" are man's search for God. But Christianity
is God's revelation of His way through Jesus Christ to struggling mankind. Once a person accepts Jesus Christ and becomes a "new creature" there is no longer any need for drugs.
And when this new Christian is filled with the Holy Spirit,
then even the power of temptation is broken, and the en-
abling power of the living Christ gives the ability to resist
the old urges forever.

Nicky

Her letter puts the finger of focus on the heart of the problem facing today's youth. Today's kids are "turned off" by
the institutional church. They are tired of "masses" and
"orders of worship" and "Sunday school parties" and dry
sermons and powerless prayers. They are fed up with what
they call "plastic preachers," men who look genuine but
have no power in their ministry. In their rebellion against
the phoniness and artificiality of the institutional church,
they have turned elsewhere for answers. They are looking for
answers in drugs, sex, demonstrations, "causes," and protest
marches. Having seen only a counterfeit picture of Jesus

Christ in the lives of those who claim to be His followers, they turn to Gandhi, Buddha, Allah, Mohammed, spiritualism, occultism, horoscopes, and Satan. At least these spirits are "real," they say (and they are), while they disclaim the Holy Spirit because they have not seen Him alive in the lives of His followers.

The answer? The only answer is a return to the ministry of the New Testament. Not just to the message (for many institutional churches have remained true to the basic Gospel message and yet the youth still walk away), but to the method. What was the New Testament method? Signs and wonders following. Healings. Miracles. Supernatural manifestations of the power of the Holy Spirit. Congregation ministry and not preacher-centered ministry.

Tragically, most institutional churches are afraid of any manifestations of the supernatural power of God. It may have been all right for Jesus to cast out demons in a loud voice, or for Paul to speak in tongues, or for Peter to heal the sick . . . but don't do it in the twentieth century, the institution says. That would shatter our serenity and might even bring the dead to life, and you know how disturbing a thing like that could be.

However, I am convinced that unless today's Christians allow the Holy Spirit to take over—unless they are baptized in the Holy Spirit, filled with the Holy Spirit—the world will never know who Jesus really is.

Therefore, I close these pages with a personal word to young people and parents. Do you want to change the world? Do you want to be filled with a power that will enable you to do miracles? Do you want your life to be characterized by such things as love, joy, peace, patience, kindness, goodness, faithfulness, gentleness, and self-control? If so, then after you have taken Jesus Christ as your Savior, receive also the Holy Spirit.

How is this done? First of all, you must possess an earnest, sincere desire to be filled. Simply saying the words with your lips is not sufficient. You must desire, from the bottom of your heart, all that God has for you.

Second, you should confess all known sin. The Bible says if we confess our sins we will be forgiven and cleansed by God. It is only the clean vessel that can be completely filled.

Third, I suggest you submit yourself completely to God. Be prepared to die as a living sacrifice. Make yourself available to God to do anything He asks of you, seeking not the gifts but the Giver.

Fourth, you must ask. Jesus said, "If you, then, bad as you are, know how to give your children what is good for them, how much more will the Heavenly Father give the Holy Spirit to those who ask Him" (Luke 11:13).

Fifth, you must believe you are filled and thank Him. One receives the Holy Spirit on faith, just as Christ is received on faith. The battle is often lost just at this point, for one can do everything else, but then fail to claim what God has given him.

Finally, you must exercise or appropriate the gifts of the Holy Spirit. These are listed (in part) in I Corinthians 12: 11-13. You must claim the power of God in you and exercise it. There can be no word of knowledge unless you speak out what God is saying. There can be no faith unless you step out on faith alone. There can be no healing unless you lay hands on the sick, and no miracles unless you invoke the power of God. There can be no prophecy unless you open your mouth or take your pen in hand, and no tongues unless you speak the sounds of praise and prayer that God gives.

Those early followers of Jesus believed all the supernatural power of God was available to them in signs and wonders, healings and miracles. However, there was a price to pay. To those men it was the price of losing their public acceptance. Whenever a miracle occurred in public (especially in the Temple) it brought persecution. They were even accused of "turning the world upside down."

When the Gospel was preached at Iconium and the "signs and wonders" exhibited, the community leaders ran the preachers out of town. That's a risk all Jesus' people have to take. And the day of stoning Christians still hasn't passed.

I challenge the young people of the world—and their parents—to forget about public opinion and become Jesus' revolutionists. You may be called a fool. You may be ridiculed. You may be called a Jesus-freak. You may be stoned. You will probably be misunderstood, especially by comfortable church members (note: I did not say "Christians" but "church members") who will accuse you of turning their world upside down.

Well, praise the Lord! I think this is the calling of today's youth—to turn this sorry world which has been almost destroyed by a blaspheming generation of adults—upside down.

In the process, some will realize that you aren't turning the world upside down—but turning it right side up. And I believe if anyone on earth can do it, it is the youth of today, filled with the Holy Spirit and marching on in the name of Jesus Christ.

If you wish to share in the work of Outreach for Youth or if you need counseling write to:

Nicky Cruz
OUTREACH
Raleigh, N.C. 27611

Ask for the booklet, "Nicky Cruz
Gives the Facts on Drugs"

Be sure to read
Nicky Cruz's life story in
Run Baby Run

Published by Logos International, Plainfield, N.J.

NICKY'S HOME DURING *Run Baby Run* DAYS.

NICKY AND GLORIA

The Cruz Family

The
little
Cruzes

An informal conversation with Billy Graham.

Nicky and Art Linkletter on location for TV Documentary, "No Need To Hide."

Nicky Cruz speaks to 9000 at 1970 Regional FGBMFI Youth Crusade, William

Now you can hear
famous authors
. . . recorded live

CASSETTES AVAILABLE

. . . telling of a personal
experience or testimony

TA 1 NICKY CRUZ, author of "RUN BABY RUN" and "THE LONELY NOW".
TA 2 (LTC) MERLIN CAROTHERS, author of "PRISON TO PRAISE".
TA 3 JAMIE BUCKINGHAM, co-author of "RUN BABY RUN", "BEN ISRAEL", "THE LONELY NOW" and others.
TA 4 ARTHUR KATZ, author of "BEN ISRAEL".
TA 5 DENNIS BENNETT, author of "NINE O'CLOCK IN THE MORNING".
TA 6 BOB BARTLETT, author of "THE SOUL PATROL."
TA 7 DR. RAY JARMAN, author of "THE GRACE AND THE GLORY OF GOD".
TA 8 MICHAEL HARPER, author of "WALK IN THE SPIRIT" and "SPIRITUAL WARFARE".
TA 9 BOB MUMFORD, author of "15 STEPS OUT".
TA10 DR. HOBART FREEMAN, author of "ANGELS OF LIGHT?"
TA11 DAVID DU PLEISSIS, author of "THE SPIRIT BADE ME GO".
TA12 WENDELL WALLACE, author of "BORN TO BURN".
TA13 DR. HOWARD ERVIN, author of "THESE ARE NOT DRUNKEN AS YE SUPPOSE".
TA14 CLINTON WHITE, author of "WISE UP! HOW?"
TA15 DR. ROBERT FROST, author of "AGLOW WITH THE SPIRIT" and "OVERFLOWING LIFE".
TA16 DR. J. RODMAN WILLIAMS, author of "THE ERA OF THE SPIRIT".
TA17 SONNY ARGUINZONI, author of "GOD'S JUNKIE".

— SPECIAL CASSETTES —

TA18 KATHRYN KUHLMAN, "AN HOUR WITH KATHRYN KUHLMAN"
TA19 KEVIN RANAGHAN, author of "CATHOLIC PENTECOSTALS".
TA20 CHARLES SIMPSON, "A SOUTHERN BAPTIST LOOKS AT PENTECOST".
TA21 WILLARD CANTELON, "THE NEW WORLD MONEY SYSTEM".
TA23 FR. JOSEPH ORSINI, "HEAR MY CONFESSION".

**LOGOS TAPES FIT ALL STANDARD CASSETTE PLAYERS . . .
EVERY LOGOS TAPE IS SOLD WITH A LIFE TIME GUARANTEE.**

3.95 each

order from your local bookstore
or CHARISMA BOOKS
Box 292
Watchung, N. J. 07061

THE SOUL PATROL by Bob Bartlett A-500/95c
A gripping account of teen challenge in Philadelphia, its birth and outreach to addicts, dropouts and problem youth.

BORN TO BURN by Wendell Wallace with Pat King A-508/95c
Pastor of a multi-racial church speaks out on the issues of today.

PSEUDO-CHRISTIANS by Dr. Ray Jarman A-516/95c
The dangers of liberal and occult teaching on lives of Christians and non-christians. Dr. Jarman for 50 years was a leader in science-of-the-mind religions until a dramatic conversion at 70 years of age.

THIS EARTH'S END by Carmen Benson A-513/95c
The Bible contains prophecy telling how this earth will end. This is a clearly written, easy to understand explanation of dreams and visions in the New Testament.

JESUS AND ISRAEL by Carmen Benson A-514/95c
The Old Testament revealed through dreams and visions the future happenings on the earth . . . an account of things to come.

WALK IN THE SPIRIT by Michael Hayes L-319/95c
Renewal or revolution - the church must decide. Some have discovered a new dimension in living through God's power.

GONE IS SHADOWS CHILD by Jessie Foy L-337/95c
A moving story of a mother's faith in God for her son and of a highly effective bio-chemical treatment called "megavitamin for schizophrenia."

SPIRITUAL WARFARE A-505/95c
A practical study of demon oppression and exorcism . . . a positive method in freeing the oppressed.

GOD'S JUNKIE by Sonnie Arguinzoni with Jorunn Rickets, introduction by David Wilkerson A-509/95c
A former junkie (his story is in Run Baby Run) tells of the unique *Addict* Church . . . "Miracles Do Happen" . . . Nicky Cruz

HEAR MY CONFESSION by Fr. Joseph E. Orsini L-341/95c
A Roman Catholic priest tells his personal story of how he discovered the Catholic Pentecostal experience.

THE LONELY NOW by Nicky Cruz with Jamie Buckingham A-510/95c
Nicky answers the questions youth ask.

RUN BABY RUN by Nicky Cruz L-101/95c
The true story of a gang leader turned crusader.

THE CHALLENGING COUNTERFEIT by Raphael Gasson L-102/95c
Hidden secrets of spiritualism disclosed by a former medium who tells how to know the real.

ANGELS OF LIGHT? by Dr. Hobart Freeman A-506/95c
Dr. Freeman reveals the source of power in the popular occult practices and the deliverence from them.

EMOTIONAL ILLS AND THE CHRISTIAN by G. J. Guldseth, M. D. A-507/95c
A high percentage of illness is attributed to the psychosomatic. Dr. Guldseth discusses ways of healing through the Bible.

PRISON TO PRAISE by Chaplain (LTC) M. Carothers A-504/95c
Revolutionary concepts in achieving remarkable answers to problems through praise.

THE SPIRIT BADE ME GO by David duPlessis L-325/95c
A charismatic journey of one man bringing him before thousands in a worldwide ecumenical mission for the Holy Spirit.

WISE UP! HOW? by Clinton White L-318/95c
"I was an alcoholic fourteen years and addicted to drugs. I was set free. I call it a miracle."

THE LONELY NOW
Special Cloth Edition $3.95